Bunyan the Christian

Bunyan the Christian

GORDON WAKEFIELD

HarperCollins*Religious*

The United Library
Garrett-Evangelical/Seabury-Western Seminaries
2121 Sheridan Road
Evanston, IL 60201

HarperCollins*Religious*
Part of HarperCollins*Publishers*
77–85 Fulham Palace Road, London W6 8JB

First published in Great Britain
in 1992 by HarperCollins*Religious*

1 3 5 7 9 10 8 6 4 2

Printed and bound in Great Britain by
HarperCollinsManufacturing Glasgow

ISBN 0 00 215 995–3

To
John Harley Lang
Dean of Lichfield

Contents

Acknowledgements

The groundwork of this book is the essay I contributed to the symposium *John Bunyan: Conventicle and Parnassus*, edited by N. H. Keeble (Clarendon Press, 1988), which I delivered also as a plenary lecture to a Bunyan Conference at Hatfield College, Durham in March 1988. This volume is the product of further reading and reflection and is, naturally, much enlarged. It follows a chronological not a thematic order. But most of the paragraphs of the essay find a home here, especially in Chapter 9, and I am grateful to the Clarendon Press for allowing me to reproduce them.

I have raided unblushingly, though always, I trust, with due acknowledgement, the latest Bunyan scholarship, which in recent years has appeared in a constant stream. The Oxford editions of Bunyan's works, not least the *Miscellaneous Works* under the general editorship of the late Professor Roger Sharrock, with their scholarly introductions, have been beside me whenever possible. I have drawn heavily on the other contributions to *John Bunyan: Conventicle and Parnassus*; and Neil Keeble's own fine study of *The Literary Culture of Nonconformity in Later Seventeenth-Century England* (Leicester University Press, 1987) has been much in my mind. Christopher Hill's prize-winning, *A Turbulent, Seditious and Factitious People: John Bunyan and his Church* (Clarendon Press, 1988), is a definitive and comprehensive work with a sensitive theological as well as political understanding and I have used it frequently. Two books published in 1991 are of interest and importance: the first volume of Isabel Rivers, *Reason, Grace and Sentiment: a study of the language of religion and ethics in England 1600–1780* (Cambridge University Press); and John Stachniewski, *The Persecutory Imagination: English puritanism and the literature of religious despair* (Clarendon Press). The latter was published as my typescript was due at HarperCollins; but Stachniewski's book is at once so fascinating and so provocative, written by an author clearly not in sympathy with the Puritans and imbued with the latest theories of historical and literary criticism, that I felt reference to it to be essential.

Other debts go back to my childhood home; to Wesley House, Cambridge, just after the Second World War; to the Principal, R. Newton Flew; to the tutor W. F. Flemington, who died, full of years, as the book was being finished; and, not least, to the late Professor Gordon Rupp, to whom, to my pleasure, Stachniewski refers as witty and stimulating on Bunyan – and supremely so on Luther as on everything else. No pupil and friend of Rupp's could write on church history without his memory and his influence falling across the pages. And there is the long affection and influence of Dr G. F. Nuttall.

There have been many other influential books and friendships, direct and indirect. The work has allowed me to acknowledge my Nonconformist loyalties, not always part of my 'image'. And I cannot forbear to mention those whose work on spirituality I happened to have been supervising in the course of composition. My wife, Beryl, has been of immense moral support and has done many of the chores of preparation with her unfailing competence. That the work passes her critical scrutiny both astonishes and reassures me. What the recipient of the dedication will make of it, I know not, but I offer it in gratitude for a friendship which in the years since we came to Lichfield has been both support and delight.

Gordon S. Wakefield
Lichfield, June 1991

1
Introduction

When I was very young, before I went to school, I would ask my mother to fasten a cushion to my back and I would wander round the kitchen of our terraced house until I came to the step which divided it from the living-room. I would expect her to stand on the step and pull me up. I was Christian with his burden, setting out on pilgrimage from the City of Destruction to the Celestial City and the step was the wicket-gate through which he entered the way. He needed "the pull" because there was danger that an arrow shot from Beelzebub's Castle, which over-looked the gate, might kill him before he had properly started on the heavenly road.

I would regale our neighbourhood walks, then on the outskirts of our Cheshire town, with Bunyan allusions, pointing out the sites of pilgrimage in the meadows, streams and houses of the lanes on which suburbia was already encroaching, using Bunyan's language with an infant memory which I doubt if I could equal now. There were days when I lived *The Pilgrim's Progress*.

Such was its influence in a Wesleyan Methodist home of the 1920s. My father, a metal machinist in the works of the London, Midland and Scottish Railway, with possibly less formal education than Bunyan himself, would chuckle over the minor characters and apply them to his acquaintances. His favourites were Mr By-ends and his relatives, particularly Mr Facing-Both-Ways. By-ends himself claims that he has "become a Gentleman of Good Quality; yet my Great-Grandfather was but a Water-man, looking one way and Rowing another; and I got most of my estate by the same occupation".

The Pilgrim's Progress has been the all-time best-seller of English Protestant spirituality. Like the greatest of such works, Dante's *Divine Comedy*, or the *Spiritual Exercises* of Ignatius Loyola, it has transcended denominational divisions. Anglo-Catholics have preached and taught courses on

1

it; Henri Talon, a French Roman Catholic, wrote a fine life of Bunyan; Cardinal Basil Hume called his collection of 1984 *To be a Pilgrim*, and prefaced it with Mr Valiant-for-Truth's hymn in the original, not the Dearmer bowdlerisation:

> Who would true valour see,
> Let him come hither.

Yet it would seem to speak less to our time than the *Revelations of Divine Love* of Julian of Norwich or Ignatian spirituality; or even the experience of St John of the Cross, with his lyrical poetry and tortuous prose; and, not least significantly, brilliant modern interpreters.[1]

Bunyan has long fascinated literary scholars.[2] He writes at the watershed between medieval allegory and the modern novel. He has not escaped the attentions of the "deconstructionalists."[3] Does this mean, in Christopher Hill's words, that "Just as Oliver Cromwell aimed to bring about the Kingdom of God on earth and founded the British Empire, so Bunyan wanted the millenium and got the novel"?[4]

It might seem so. Yet, as may be adduced from Hill, liberation theologians might claim him. *The Pilgrim's Progress* is set among the common ways of Bedfordshire, the street corners with their gossip, the muddy lanes and fields, the sloughs and snares, the great houses, which Bunyan would know only from the servant's entrance. Its bias is to the poor. Its evil characters are mostly gentlemen or women; and we may discern social protest in the succession of Lollards and Levellers, in an age when religion and politics were one. In Part II, Great-heart slays Giant Grim, or Bloody-Man, who may be identified with Judge Jeffreys but who also blocks the King's Highway by enclosure. In the altercations before the killing Christiana speaks as a "Mother in Israel", like Deborah, demanding passage for the pilgrims. Christopher Hill has written of the wide sales of *The Pilgrim's Progress* in the Third World, while:

> In the 1850s and early 1960s the Taiping rebels came very near to conquering the whole of China; nearer than any other nineteenth-century rebellion. They drew in hundreds of millions of people. The Taiping were a radical Christian sect, who strongly emphasized hymn-singing, and made the Ten Commandments their basic disciplinary code. Their leader, Hong Xiuquan, called his capital (Nanjing) the New Jerusalem. His two favourite books were the Bible and *The Pilgrim's Progress*. If the Taiping had won, Bunyan's allegory might have become China's earlier little red book.[5]

Hill and E. P. Thompson are right to connect Bunyan's writings with political and social events, even to detect a "slumbering radicalism" and the embryo of later working-class movements,[6] though the effect of *The Pilgrim's Progress* in Nonconformist homes was not to encourage revolution. There was a clear judgement on the worldly and the oppressors. There might well be support for political agitation and movements for social reform. But Greatheart's sword was of the Spirit and the goal of all warfare and strife was the kingdom that transcends this world and the city beyond our mortal life, whose maker and builder is God. It may well be that the great allegory, like Milton's three epics, was composed partly to come to terms with the failure of "the good old cause", sealed by the Restoration, to accept, with sorrowful reluctance, a hierarchical system intermittently cruel and always discriminatory against dissent, which could not bring the New Jerusalem down from heaven into England's green and pleasant land; and this, while protesting against injustice and "worldliness", the licentiousness and debauchery of the ruling classes. But Bunyan's Christian faith is not simply a code for social change, nor his theology covert politics. He may call in the eternal order to redress the balance of the temporal, and see the heavenly city beyond death as the reward and recompense for the oppression and ills of all earthly systems. This has long been out of fashion and much scorned. It has been caricatured and contemned as much by Christians as sceptics. It may have made people acquiesce too easily in the injustices and imperfections of human society, reluctant to campaign for its reformation when they could. But wherein otherwise is their hope and happiness, apart from the ephemeral adrenalin and mortal associations which sustain our life and optimism in this world? Revolutions never succeed completely and Utopianism may cause worse ills than it seeks to transcend.

Has Bunyan's religion any meaning for our time, the nuclear age, the one world of technology, of the free market and the enterprise culture, the life which to the western secularist, who has much influenced the churches, is all? As a child I did not yawn over the theological discourses of *The Pilgrim's Progress* but passed them over with uncomprehending respect. It was the journey, the incidents and the characters which captured my imagination, as my father's. The Edinburgh preacher Alexander Whyte (1836–1921) lectured on Bunyan characters and not only those from *The Pilgrim's Progress*.[7] He was of amazingly Catholic sympathies, interpreter of Teresa of Avila, Andrewes, Boehme, Thomas Browne, and William Law. He revered Newman, and caused controversy by some Marian sermons. Yet Puritan theology had excited him from early years, though in its tenderer aspects, as in Samuel Rutherford. He thought that the Puritan divine, Thomas Goodwin, chaplain to Cromwell, should have a prominent place in the curriculum of the Free Church of Scotland ministerial students. It is significant that Goodwin provided Protestant devotion to the Sacred Heart of Jesus, then a popular, rather carnal cult in Roman Catholic France, in his treatise, "The Heart of Christ in Heaven towards Sinners on Earth". The rigours were softened. And, for Whyte, the discourses in Bunyan were no desiccated scholasticism, the arid logic-chopping of predestinarians wrestling with their election. Often conducted with tears, they spoke of the eternal verities and consolations of faith. Even so, Henri Talon has some justification for complaining that Whyte is "the most guilty of those who crush charming sketches under the weight of forced commentaries".[8]

My own first book, *Puritan Devotion*, is still sometimes referred to, and is a modest contribution to the large attempt from both sides of the Atlantic to rehabilitate puritanism and redeem it from the obloquy of popular and ecclesiastical misrepresentation. Today the study would need to be more discriminating in the light of the work of Patrick Collinson, Basil Hall, Neil Keeble and others. It suffers from the tendency to which Free Churchmen in particular have been prone, to describe all who were opposed to the Acts of Uniformity from Elizabeth I to Charles II as Puritans. It is now clear that the name should properly apply to those, mostly Calvinist in theology, who sought to reform the English Church from within. Puritans were not separatists. The nickname was an insult, with its echoes of the medieval *Cathari* and its precisionist sound. It branded those of a strict and devout life who questioned the state settlement but were not wholly opposed to the liturgy of the Book of Common Prayer of 1552, done as Cranmer intended it without Catholic appurtenances. It seemed to pass from use after 1642 to be replaced by party names – Presbyterian, Independent, Anabaptist, and in time many others. Should Bunyan strictly be called a Puritan? In *The Life and Death of Mr Badman*, Mr Wiseman describes someone as "a godly old Puritan, for so the godly were called in time past", though it should be remembered that this work was published in 1680, long after the conflicts which led to war, or for that matter the Restoration. There had been many changes by then. And it is doubtful if in our time we can avoid using Puritan as an umbrella term. We must distinguish different types and developments of puritanism, as Dr Nuttall did in what stands as a definitive work, *The Holy Spirit in Puritan Faith and Experience* (1946). But he writes:

Some of the Episcopalians within the Established Church, all the

4

Presbyterians and Independents within it before 1662, most of the Separatist and sectarian leaders outside it, and the founders of Nonconformity after 1662, are thus all spiritually nearer to one another than is any of them to the Roman Catholic Church or to the Laudian party within the Church of England. They have their own internal differences, some of them sharp . . . but in a large sense they have much in common, and for this faith and experience which they share . . . there is no other name than Puritan.[9]

The common characteristics of puritanism in this comprehensive sense were:

1 An intensely personal religious experience and sense of call.
2 A conviction of the necessity of conversion, though, in Baxter's words, "God breaketh not all men's hearts alike".
3 Federal theology; all rests on the Divine Covenant.
4 A life of moral seriousness, though not wholly lacking in a sense of humour or awareness of the arts, especially music.
5 A profound concern with "casuistry", that is, the resolution of "cases of conscience", often dealt with in the pulpit. This was shared with the Caroline divines.[10]

Recently I have been invited to treat of Anglican spirituality.[11] I find myself at home there, though it partakes in part of "the new prelatical way" of Baxter's stricture and Bunyan's ardent dislike, from which both suffered. It has beauty and order, a sense of oneness with the historic and holy tradition and of the awesomeness of things unseen. But I am still haunted by the Puritans and the extremer sects, who, in spite of those characteristics both open to caricature and to the charge of theological cruelty, had deep, indeed desperate, dedication and pastoral tenderness, and cannot be ignored in "the great Church". And I offer this theological biography of John Bunyan in the hope that something in his understanding of the ways of God may speak to our condition. This may warn us against a too-superficial unity, which ignores the essential dialectic of Church relations. Far more, it may give some insight into the mystery of our religion and the greatness of redeeming love.

2
Early Life and Times

There were many Bunyans in Bedfordshire in the seventeenth century and they had been there a long time. The name may be of French origin and they possibly came over at the Conquest.

John Bunyan belonged to the lower orders, the "downstairs" of society, and was a tinker or brazier, the son of a tinker, a trade of the large class of "mechanics", which included a good many of the rascally sort. This was due to his family's decline, for in the mid-sixteenth century the Bunyans had farmed nine acres around Elstow, and there were fields known as "Bunyans" and "Farther Bunyans" as well as a Bunyans Walk and Bunyans End. His father, Thomas, at least the third in succession of that name, lived from 1603 to 1676. He was always among the poor. John was the child of the second of his three wives, born in November 1628 at Elstow, Bedford, the precise date not known. In spite of poverty, John went to school, possibly the Grammar School at Houghton Conquest, and learned to read and write. He doubtless left early and regarded his lack of a classical education, which later led his judges to think him overbold in becoming a preacher, as a supreme qualification in that he spoke and wrote from Scripture and experience and not from authorities and tradition.

He was right, but disingenuous none the less; for he was very much the product of a counter-culture, powerful and learned in its own way: its power was religion and its learning the Bible.

He did not receive this culture from his home. His father was not a Puritan and does not seem to have entered into his son's faith. At his first stirrings of religion, John, so he tells us, started to go to church twice a day. He seems to have been a Laudian of sorts, though this was probably some years after the Archbishop's execution. He revered the Church, its ministers, "the High-Place, Priest, Clerk, Vestments, Service and what else",[1] all of which he was soon to scorn. He owed his encounters with religious diversity chiefly to the civil wars of the 1640s. These brought the wider world to bucolic Bedfordshire and its lace-manufacturing county town, population 2000, for there were skirmishes on the bridge, and in 1645 Cromwell and his armies passed through. Military service would expose the young man to the ferment of religious and political debate, which the very assembling of the Cromwellian army and its subsequent victory released, together with the abolition of the very severe Laudian censorship. It seems certain that he joined the Parliamentary garrison at Newport Pagnell, just over the border in Buckinghamshire. His mother had died in July 1644 and his father soon married again. A short-lived son was born within months and christened the royal name of Charles, which, says Christopher Hill, may have been provocative if John's service and sympathies were already on the Parliament side.

Bunyan seems to have been in the army for two and a half years. They were chaotic and uneasy years in the life of the nation. Parliament's victory was secured within months of his enlistment, but the army was ill-paid and ill-equipped, as well as riven by a gallimaufry of political and religious notions.

Presbyterians and Independents

These were the heirs of the old Puritans of Queen Elizabeth's time, differing more in Church polity than theology, which was predominantly, though not entirely Calvinist, after the manner of the Cambridge divine William Perkins (1558–1602). English Calvinism was more Calvinist than Calvin in the matter of predestination, yet had a certain humanity and tenderness, which led some continentals, especially in the Netherlands, to dismiss it as soft. By the early 1640s these Puritans were divided into Presbyterians and Independents. The Presbyterians wished to replace the Anglican with the Genevan system, though in England they were noted more for a type of piety, evidenced by such as Richard Baxter, than for a rigid ecclesiology, and were not averse to a modified episcopacy.[2] The Independents or Congregationalists registered their objections to "Presbyteriall government" in a declaration of 1648, which affirmed the autonomy of the congregation as containing within itself the powers which under Presbyterianism subordinated it to outside courts, "Standing Synods, Provinciall, Nationall, and Oecumenical". The idea of the covenant was central both to Presbyterians and Independents, though the Presbyterian conception was of a covenant for the nation, the Independent of a covenant for each local church. This, derived from Scripture, God's covenant with Israel, and the new covenant

7

sealed by the blood of Christ, had its origin in the love, initiative and faithfulness of God and was a solemn pledge in response, on behalf of his people, binding them to observe his ordinances, follow the law of Christ and submit to him as the only governor of the Church.

Some Independents were Baptists, that is, they repudiated infant baptism. Their opponents tended to call them "ana", that is, rebaptisers, since they insisted on baptising those who had been christened as babies; but they did this because they believed that infant baptism was not true baptism. They did not dispute the once-for-allness of the valid sacrament of initiation. And there were varying degrees of rigour in this as in much else and great controversy. All believed that Church membership should be limited to "visible saints"; to be "in Christ" was the criterion rather than credal subscription, though there were some differences as to its ethical norms. The situation was complicated by the fact that while there were separate congregations formed largely by those who had returned from Carolingian exile, Presbyterians and Congregationalists also held the livings of parish and collegiate churches and the stalls of cathedrals, now administered according to the systems to which ministers and people adhered.

These, doctrinally orthodox and Trinitarian at this period, were not uninfluenced by eschatological expectations which seem strange in our time, but which are understandable in the light both of a literalist reading of Scripture (especially Revelation) and the crisis of these revolutionary years. Many moderate Christians of various persuasions had cherished millenarian hopes since the Reformation, and the overthrow of the Church, the lords, the king, in the late 1640s seemed to be the harbinger of the imminent rule of Christ and his saints on earth. But the wars ended in disillusion and bitter disagreement and an eruption of radicalism, much of it threatening violence, which alarmed the moderate majority.

Radicals

Cromwell was tolerant of heretics and subversives in his New Model Army and it was seething with radicals, though they were not confined to its ranks. What must never be forgotten is that some of the conservatives and moderates passed over the ill-defined boundaries into various forms of radicalism. This was particularly true of Baptists. And there is no doubt that Bunyan himself, in the course of the spiritual conflicts which we shall describe, was drawn to types of religion which he came vehemently to condemn.

The "left" has always been unable to present a united front, whether in politics or religion, and the various movements could not cohere or agree among themselves.

Levellers

There were the Levellers, of whom the chief was John Lilburne, who believed that Bible and statute book alike should be taken from clerics and lawyers and opened to the people, who would understand their basic simplicities, which might be summed up in the Golden Rule, "Do unto others as you would that they should do unto you". Christopher Hill has called them "Arminians of the left": they repudiated both the predominant Calvinism and its doctrine that only a few would be saved; and the "Arminianism of the right", which preached salvation through the Church and its ceremonies. Acts of love and charity rather than rituals and orders were the demand of Christ, the moral consequences of his passion. They must, fight tyranny and oppression with arms if necessary. Their bias must be to the poor. The rich and ruling were the source of evil and injustice and the worst of these were found among "professors" who were wealthy, "saints", Puritans, who had grown prosperous and whom the outcome of the wars had placed in power. They were strong in the principles of compassion, the philosophy of Christ, of liberty and equality; weak in programmes for political action, possibly because they believed that the chief requisite was a change in individual hearts.

Diggers

These were a minority most evident in the year 1649 to 1650 in Surrey and possibly not of direct concern to Bunyan, except in so far as they were part of the confused milieu of his experience. Yet they had colonies for a while at Dunstable and Wellingborough and some of them from Surrey paid a visit to Bedford in 1650. Gerrard Winstanley was their genius. His thought is too complex and too important to be summed up in a sentence or two. He was an original and creative thinker not irrelevant to our own day. It is sufficient to note that having begun with the belief that religion was a matter of inward life and not outward forms, he became convinced, partly through a trance, that it demanded a revolutionary social order, a form of communism, in which there were no rights of private property and anyone could dig anywhere. A small group proceeded to do so near Walton-on-Thames and were brutally treated by the local inhabitants. They were no more violent than the women of Greenham Common. The experiment, neither in Surrey nor in spasmodic outbreaks elsewhere, did not survive for long; but it was a sign of an alternative society. Winstanley, who lived until 1676, became a Quaker in the 1660s, returning in some sense to his original insights. As with the Levellers, there was a passionate belief that clergy and university education were the enemies of truth and justice, instruments of a hierarchical order which maintained the poor in thrall and had lost what, in our time, A. N. Whitehead was to call "the Galilean vision of humility".

Ranters and Fifth Monarchists

These concerned Bunyan far more and at one time were rivals for his allegiance, which accounts for his fierce opposition and hatred. They arose due to the disillusion caused by the suppression of the Levellers. They so frightened all the protagonists of good order in Church and State that it is difficult to distinguish just condemnation from terrified travesty. J. F. McGregor gets it right when he says, "The Ranter prophets were mystical antinomians: mystical in their claim to have become one with God; antinomian in denying the reality of sin to the believer."[3] They were enthusiasts, charismatics, who claimed to be as the Son of God while they indulged in sexual promiscuity as free of the old law contained in the Ten Commandments. Their reported orgies doubtless owe much to the fearful imagination of their foes. They were hardly precursors of the holders of twentieth-century acid-house parties. And there is no indication that, as Ranters, they conspired further revolution, though they may have had affinities with the Fifth Monarchists, so-called from Daniel 7 and his vision of the four beasts, the brutish kingdoms of the earth, overcome by the human being who comes on the clouds of heaven and represents the holy ones of the Most High whose is everlasting sovereignty. They were different from the Ranters in that they believed that the reign of King Jesus would be based on the Mosaic laws, which are an interesting combination of the humanitarian and the draconian. The Fifth Monarchists had a clearer political programme than the other radicals. They included former Congregationalists and some members of the upper classes. Their violence may have been more verbal than military, through they justified regicide both against Cromwell, whom they regarded as the greatest of traitors after he had established the Protectorate, and against Charles II. They promoted two uprisings against Protector and King respectively and were incessant propagandists and subversives.

Quakers

Of all the radical movements the Quakers were destined to be the most powerful, ubiquitous and, to the various orthodoxies, threatening. They began in the north of England and the young soldier Bunyan may not have encountered them, since their national impact has been dated from 1654/5, though George Fox had visited Newport Pagnell in 1644 and the New Model Army was a recruiting ground, as for all the radical sects. But his spiritual autobiography, and his other writings, make it clear that he regarded them as Ranters redivivi:

> the very opinions that are held att this day by the Quakers, are the same that long ago were held by the Ranters. Only the Ranters had made them thredbare at an Ale-house, and the Quakers have set a new glosse upon them again, by an outward legal holiness.[4]

They seem largely to have been drawn from the middle or lower-middle classes. They had much in common with the other radicals and represented an interesting graduation both from the Levellers and others and the orthodox Puritans. They were anti-Calvinist and universalist. The light within, the Holy Spirit or Christ in the heart – the distinctions are unclear as they always have been – was the millennium, the parousia, the coming of Christ. This had greater authority than Scripture, which might be a dead letter – a reaction against the culture of scholarship and the book. As this spread throughout humankind it would be accompanied by social change, but the kingdom of heaven was first within. They were influenced by the hermetic writings, of which, as C. H. Dodd demonstrated, the fourth evangelist was so much aware, and had "green" predilections.

The Quakers were no serene and peaceful Society of Friends. They were ecstatic enthusiasts. Their meetings could be manifestations of corporate shaking and trembling – hence their name. They were perfectionists who believed that Christ lived in them, and in at least one sad and notorious case that they were as him. They were miracle workers, claiming – and

11

revealing – the apostolic powers of the longer ending of St Mark's gospel. Like all the radicals they hated the clergy and the gentry and subscribed to the myth that privilege, class and oppression dated from the Norman Conquest. They stressed the peaceful nature of the movement rather than opposition to the use of force in all circumstances. Their pacifism from the Restoration was "forced upon them by the hostility of the outside world".[5] They gave greater prominence to women than most religious bodies and some of their agitators were female, perhaps in the succession of Jenny Geddes. They were persecuted with great barbarity, not least under the Commonwealth. Their effect, more than that of most radicals, may have been to strengthen the forces of traditionalism and make the Restoration inevitable. Their existence seemed to portend a chaotic eccentricity more to be dreaded than the tyranny of kings.

The radical movements were all popular, rising from and supported by the people, in whom they had a Utopian faith, in contrast to their deep hostility to hierarchies. But it must not be imagined that they represented a majority of the population, who were probably conservative and happiest in the old ways. They had a brief morning once the wars were over and there must have been the Wordsworthian feeling at the start of another, later revolution. "Bliss was it that dawn to be alive". By the beginning of the sixth decade of the century it must have been obvious that they could not succeed, but they continued to have potency and to attract Christians disillusioned with orthodoxy. And while the seventeenth century seems to us to be an age dominated by religion, in which every issue had religious implications and was presented in religious terms, secularism had been advancing since the Renaissance and blatant irreligion was not without its representatives.

After military service

Christopher Hill[6] has imagined in a few sentences the young Bunyan home from the army, back to tinkering and tipcat, craving perhaps the life and comradeship he had lost, no longer a callow youth, something of a "blood", ringleader of youth, doubtless sought after by the girls; but maybe not happy at home with his father's third wife, though the infant Charles was dead. Was this why he married young, though we do not know precisely when? A first daughter, the blind Mary, was baptised on 20th July 1650. We are ignorant of his wife's name – he never tells us (rather like St John omitting the name of the Mother of Jesus in his references to her). She does not seem to have been a local girl but we know that she came of a godly father; and we know her dowry:

> . . . this woman and I, though we came together as poor as poor might be (not having so much household-stuff as a Dish or Spoon betwixt us both), yet this she had for her part, The Plain Mans Pathway to Heaven, and The Practice of Piety, which her Father had left her when he died. In these two Books I should sometimes read with her, wherein I also found some things that were somewhat pleasing to me: (but all this while I met with no conviction).

The books did not convert John Bunyan, they did not reach his heart, but they kindled "some desire to religion" and were not without influence on his writing and his theology.

The Plain Man's Pathway to Heaven was published in 1601, in Amsterdam, not in England, for safety's sake. It was in its twenty-fifth edition by 1640 and went on to sell 100,000 copies by the early eighteenth century. Dent, who wrote other works of popular theology, was a strict Calvinist, a fervent believer in hell-fire, but he is not insensitive to social problems, castigates the faults of the godly as well as the wicked and writes racily. Not only is the Christian life seen as a journey but the book uses dialogue, as did Bunyan in sermons as well as in *The Pilgrim's Progress*. Dent also anticipates some of Bunyan's characterisation. It is fair to say that there would have been neither *The Pilgrim's Progress* nor *The Life and Death of Mr Badman* without *The Plain Man's Pathway*. Dent also offers, as Calvinists had to, tests by which the tortured soul can gain assurance of being right with God. He provides "Eight Infallible Notes and Tokens of a Regenerate Mind", which became part of a common Puritan stock:

1 A love to the children of God.
2 A delight in his word.
3 Fervent prayer.
4 Zeal of God's glory.
5 Denial of ourselves.
6 Patient bearing of the cross.
7 Faithfulness in our callings.
8 Just and conscionable dealings.

Isabel Rivers has contrasted both Dent's and Bayly's books with Richard Allestree's *The Practice of Christian Graces* (1658), better known by its subtitle *The Whole Duty of Man*, which "effectively replaced them to become the most popular and influential religious work in the late seventeenth century and throughout the eighteenth". She says, "Where Dent and Bayly stress election and regeneration (and the fruits that follow), Allestree stresses fulfilment of duty and holiness of life as the condition on which the promises are given".[7] To the Calvinist this is sheer legalism, Moses brought in and not even by the back door.

Lewis Bayly's *The Practice of Piety* (1612) was to be even more widespread in its provenance than *The Plain Man's Pathway*. It had reached its twenty-fifth edition by 1630, its fifty-ninth in 1735, and was last reissued in 1842. It was translated into French in 1625, Welsh in 1630, German in 1629, Polish in 1647; and in 1665 at Cambridge, Mass. it was turned into the tongue of the local Indians.

Bayly himself, who became Bishop of Bangor, lived dangerously. He avoided public disgrace and humiliation, yet scandal accompanied him and scurrilous gossip from first to last. He knew royal favour, yet constantly jeopardised it through tactlessness; his book was not approved in court circles, while some Puritans were suspicious of it, but worse, in 1626 he was accused before the House of Commons on charges, "which endorsed by Laud, and 'palpably proved' in Parliament, included every kind of misdemeanor from licensing promiscuity in others to practising it himself".[8] It was even said that he had filched *The Practice of Piety* from the widow of its true author, a Puritan minister, and, with a few interpolations, published it as his own.

The treatise does not presuppose the poverty of a Bunyan. It is written for the householder, the man of business and of property, who administers his family and domestics as the preacher does the congregation and calls them together each day for prayer. The practice of piety is a seventeenth-century term for what we would call spirituality. Bayly grounds it solidly in Calvinist theology. It begins with God and the awesome, inscrutable yet loving purpose of God in Christ. Response to this, the making sure of calling and election, is in a life of ordered prayer, worship and good works, of which Sunday, kept very much according to the Jewish Sabbath – a Puritan departure from original Protestantism to which it was alien – is the pivot. More space is devoted to Holy Communion, interpreted in the Western and Prayer Book tradition as essentially a memorial of Christ's death, than to any other theme. Many of the meditations are from the common stock of Puritan spirituality and, interestingly, are derived from Juan Luis Vives or Ludovicus (1492–1540), a Roman Catholic who taught briefly in Oxford. Everyday tasks must be accompanied by thoughts of our last and chief end. The bed is always to remind the sleeper of his grave, his rising of the resurrection from the dead. Should he hear the cock crow he must remember Peter's denial and penitence with many tears. The putting on of clothes is to carry the mind back to our primeval innocence and fallen shame. The sun streaming through the windows is to be a sign of the Sun of righteousness risen with healing in his wings. The book concludes with "The Soul's Soliloquie ravished in contemplation of the Passion of Our Lord". This is an English version of the prayer *Quid commisisti dulcissime puer, ut sic iudicaris*, attributed to St Augustine, and found in the writings of the eleventh-century Archbishop of Canterbury, St Anselm. It is also paraphrased in the German hymn of Johann Heermann (1585–1647), translated by Robert Bridges: "Ah, holy Jesu, how hast thou offended/That man to judge thee hath in hate pretended?" Archdeacon Stranks singled out this post-Communion prayer as central to Bayly's type of spirituality:

Therefore, O Father, for the bitter death and bloody Passion's sake which thy Son Jesus Christ has suffered for me, and I have now remembered unto thee: pardon and forgive thou unto me all my Sins, and deliver me from the Curse and Vengeance which they have justly deserved, and through his Merits, make me, O Lord, a partaker of Thy Mercy.[9]

The dark valley

For Bunyan's early life we rely on his spiritual autobiography *Grace Abounding to the Chief of Sinners*. This creates problems. It was published in 1666 and written in prison more than a decade after the experiences it describes; and, as Christopher Hill says, "The chronology is at best imprecise, at worst chaotic . . . It is almost impossible to establish the sequence of events".[10] Had Bunyan, like many Puritans, kept a private diary of his years of spiritual agony, it might have read differently from his retrospective account, within which, as Vincent Newey has said, there are two Bunyans. There is his past self which he recreates and the present author who tells the story for his own and others' benefit.[11]

Yet this does not necessarily militate against the accuracy of the record; retrospection may enhance it. Peter Brown, in the chapter on "The Confessions" in his life of Augustine of Hippo, recognises that a book contemporary with Augustine's conversion might have been much more circumstantial, but it might not have "conveyed so insistently" his life of feeling

15

both before and after the moments in the Milan Garden.[12] Similarly with the very different Bunyan and his very different autobiography, different in cultural background, in learning, in theological interests, in style and in pathology though it is in the Augustinian succession.

Grace Abounding may seem at first glance to belong to the genre of Puritan and radical conversion narratives and to follow the pattern Roger Sharrock has outlined – early providential mercies, unregenerate life, calling and conversion, often followed by a vocation to preach and an account of the ministry.[13] But it is a far from conventional work for two reasons.

First there is the literary genius of the author, manifest in his amazing gift of expression, vivid, Anglo-Saxon, lyrical; but also in the ability Charles Peguy ascribed to Victor Hugo of seeing creation as if she had come that morning from the hands of the Creator.[14] He has what Richard Greaves has described in words which almost reduce Bunyan to scholarship, "an intuitive contemporaneity with the events he proclaimed from the pulpit".[15] This is illustrated in one of the most moving passages of *Grace Abounding*:

> . . . me thought I was as if I had seen him born, as if I had seen him grow up, as if I had seen him walk thorow this world, from the Cradle to his cross; to which also when he came, I saw how gently he gave himself to be hanged and nailed on it for my sins and wicked doings; also as I was musing on this his progress, that dropped on my spirit, he was ordained for the slaughter, 1 Peter 1:19–20. When I have considered the truth of his resurrection, and have remembered that word, Touch me not Mary etc., I have seen as if he leapt at the Grave's mouth for joy that he was risen again and had got the conquest over our dreadful foes, John 20: 1–17. I have also in the spirit seen him a man on the right hand of God the Father for me, and have seen the manner of his coming from Heaven to judge the world with glory.[16]

Second, there is the question of Bunyan's psychological and mental state. Was he during the years the autobiography describes on the verge of insanity? The relation between religious experience and schizophrenia is demanding and undergoing investigation. We have known people of amazing religious gifts, perceptions and intuitions, awareness of the reality of God, who have lived on an abyss of insanity into which they have sometimes fallen. The Latin phrase "*Quem Deus vult perdere, prius dementat*" "Whom God wills to destroy he first drives mad", which originated in a scholastic's quotation of an unknown poet in commentary on Sophocles's

Antigone, has been reformulated to read "*Quem Deus vult salvare . . .* "
"Whom God wills to *save* he first drives mad".[17]

But what is madness? We might define it as inability to live in the world
of normal human relationships, removal from what we regard as reality,
solid, concrete, earthy, into the sphere of hallucinations and manifesting
itself in eccentric and sometimes violent and dangerous behaviour. It may
include the psychological state of manic depression, though this in itself is
not insanity.

There are varying degrees of madness and it is sometimes closely connec-
ted with genius. It is related to obsessiveness. An obsession may drive a
person mad; on the other hand may it not be a symptom of pre-existent
madness? The philosopher Ludwig Wittgenstein formed close friendships
and though sometimes moody and exasperating was often a more than
tolerable companion. But his eccentricity made people describe him as mad.
Was this because his constant and relentless pursuit of logic unbalanced his
brain? Or would only a madman be so besotted with logic? One characteristic of Wittgenstein's personal relationships was his perpetual analysis of
his friends, not clinically but in conversation. But this was as nothing to his
preoccupation with himself. Long evenings with Bertrand Russell would be
spent in:

> discussing himself as much as logic. He would, according to Russell,
> "pace up and down my room like a wild beast for three hours in
> agitated silence". Once, Russell asked: "Are you thinking about logic
> or your sins?" "Both," Wittgenstein replied, and continued his pacing.
> Russell, his patience temporarily exhausted by weeks of this kind of
> thing, told Wittgenstein that he thought too much about himself.[18]

John Bunyan does not seem to have behaved with peculiar eccentricity
to outward view or wearied his friends with his broodings over his inward
states, though he took his problems to them from time to time. After all,
he lived among those who were as concerned as he was about their sins
and sought salvation. The Philippian gaoler's question, "What must I do
to be saved?" was a basic premise of their lives. All serious men and
women were worried about their acceptance at the last and lived in a
spiritual universe constructed from medieval models of heaven and hell
and the day of doom, reinforced since the Reformation with the threats
and promises of Scripture. But in the depths of his heart there were
fightings and fears, strivings and struggles of the spiritual genius near
breakdown rather than the conventional entrant into conversion, which he

confessed only to a few and kept much to himself until he wrote his autobiography years later.

The inward torments he suffered go back to his childhood. He says that even when a small boy he had "but few equals . . . both for cursing, swearing, lying and blaspheming the holy Name of God".[19] These transgressions in the day were followed in the night by fearful dreams of devils seeking to take him away with them, and of hell-fire. Yet he did not reform and in adolescence the dreams left him, so that until his marriage he was "the very ring-leader of all the Youth that kept me company, into all manner of vice and ungodliness."[20] In the light of this it is puzzling that a presumably respectable young woman, daughter of a good Puritan, was willing to marry him. There is no evidence that he had got her with child.

Impenitent and dissolute as he was, he could not bear to see wickedness on the part of those who professed goodness and to hear such a person swear caused him heartache. He believed also that God had not deserted him but intervened to preserve his life when he fell into "a crick of the sea", and another time out of a boat into the Ouse at Bedford. One incident, cited as testimony of God's providential care, shows something of his vehemence and passion:

It chanced that an adder passed over the highway, so I having a stick in mine hand, struck her over the back; and having stounded (stunned) her, I forced open her mouth with my stick, and plucked her sting out with my fingers, by which act had not God been merciful to me. I might by my desperateness have brought myself to mine end.[21]

His most notable escape was when, during his time in the army, another soldier at the last minute asked leave to replace him on a foray and was killed.

His wife's dowry and her reminiscences of her father, as we have seen, turned him towards religion. He did not, as so many of like disposition, refuse to read the books or simply scoff. He became a formal churchgoer bedazzled with the appurtenances of religion, bemused at times over things he heard from Scripture about the Israelites, for instance, the people of God. Calvinism was in the air and he wondered, "Whether we were of the Israelites or no." He asked his father, who must have taken him literally and answered, "No, we were not." But he had no conviction of sin, nor thought of Christ the only Saviour. A sermon against Sabbath-breaking pricked his conscience, but, after a good dinner, he "shook the sermon out of (his) mind" and went out to play.

It was that very afternoon when he was playing tipcat, a game which seems to be the origin of both baseball and cricket, and was about to cudgel the wood a second time that a voice seemed suddenly to dart from heaven into his soul and say *Wilt thou leave thy sins and go to heaven? or have thy sins and go to hell?* This arrested him but brought him to such consciousness of sin that he was in total despair and therefore continued the more vigorously in his worldly course. Damned either way, he might as well "be damned for many sins as few".

A month or so later he was cursing before a shop window, just for the very devil of it, and his language was so foul that the woman inside, though "a loose and ungodly wretch", trembled at the sound and told him that he was the ungodliest fellow for swearing that she had ever heard in her life and a corrupter of youth. This rebuke silenced him and to his amazement purged his lips and made him speak civilly without oaths and obscenities. But he continued with his sports.

Then he fell in with a poor man "that made profession of religion" and "talked pleasantly of the Scriptures". So Bunyan started to read the Bible and enjoyed it, especially the history, but he "could not away" with Paul's Epistles and the like. He did not really understand the nature of sin nor of Christ's salvation.

He tried to keep the commandments and his neighbours thought him converted. He gave up bell-ringing out of fear that the bells should fall on him, or, if he stood outside in the churchyard to listen, the tower might collapse. Gradually he ceased from dancing, though the joy of it remained in his Christian soul, as *The Pilgrim's Progress* is evidence. He considered himself a good man, though "was nothing but a poor painted hypocrite". His direst conflicts were just beginning. It is somewhat ironic that for the Protestant evangelical to attain salvation by faith meant a harder road than salvation by works, and a life and death battle of which the simply good and conscientious had no knowledge.

One day, going about his tinker's work in a Bedford street, he came upon "three or four poor women sitting at a door in the Sun and talking about the things of God". They pointed to a dimension of Christian experience out of Bunyan's reach. They spoke of new birth, of the love of God in Christ to refresh and support them. They told of manifold temptations "and did contemn, slight and abhor their own righteousness, as filthy and insufficient to do them good. And methought they spake as if joy did make them speak."[22]

Bunyan went frequently into these poor people's company; but though he loved to be with them and found them irresistible, they made him question his condition the more.

He had a remarkable vision at this time in which he saw his poor people of Bedford:

as if they were set on the Sunny side of some pleasant Mountain, there refreshing themselves with the pleasant beams of the Sun, while I was shivering and shrinking in the cold, afflicted with frost, snow and dark clouds; methought also betwixt me and them I saw a wall that did compass about this Mountain; now thorow this wall my Soul did greatly desire to pass, concluding that if I could, I would go even into the very midst of them, and there also comfort myself with the heat of their Sun.

After much searching he found a narrow gap "like a little doorway in the wall". It was strait and narrow indeed and Bunyan could hardly inch himself through, but in the end, after a prodigious effort, he did so, and with great gladness, "went and sat down in the midst of them, and so was comforted with the light and heat of their Sun".

The interpretation was not difficult. The sun was the glory and grace of God, the mountain the church, the narrow gate, Christ. The struggle to enter it might almost seem to deny salvation by faith and imply that by immense effort does one enter the fellowship of the redeemed. And Bunyan, like any Caroline divine, is convinced that salvation means a renunciation of the world, which may be painful; "for here was only roome for Body and Soul, but nott for Body and Soul and Sin".[23] But Bunyan is not like the man waiting at Kafka's narrow door which closes for ever before he can gain admittance.

The vision did not, however, bring him assurance or indeed much consolation. We will not follow paragraph by paragraph his agonised vicissitudes, but instead notice some of the stations and the snares of his pilgrim way.

Here is a nature, tender and passionate, made the more so by his trials and his encounter with the poor women of Bedford. He has a love and longing for Christ; hence his agony. Only a lover could know his scruples, doubts and uncertainties, be tormented by a conscience so sensitive and bruised as his. He heard a sermon from the Song of Solomon 4:1, "Behold thou art fair, my Love; behold thou art fair." He remembers the five points:

1 That the Church, and so every saved soul, is Christ's love, when loveless.
2 Christ's love without a cause.
3 Christ's love when hated of the world.
4 Christ's love when under temptation and under dissertion.
5 Christ's love from first to last.

This exposition may be paralleled in much seventeenth-century divinity, such as Dean Samuel Crossman's hymn "Love unknown": "Love to the loveless shown/that they might lovely be." For Bunyan it was the fourth particular of the sermon which warmed his heart: "If it be so, that the saved soul is Christ's love when under temptation and dissertion; then poor tempted Soul, when thou art assaulted and afflicted with temptation, and the hidings of God's face, yet think on these two words, MY LOVE, still."

On his way home the words began to kindle in his heart, "Thou art my love, thou art my love." For a while he was in a rapture of joy as he repeated them and linked them with the promise of Romans 8 that nothing can separate us from God's love in Christ. He wondered how he could contain this till he got home:

> I thought I could have spoken of his Love, and of his mercy to me,
> even to the very Crows that sat upon the plow'd lands before me,
> had they been capable to understand me, wherefore I said in my Soul
> with much gladness, Well, I would I had a pen and ink here, I would
> write this down before I go any further, for surely I will not forget
> *this* forty years hence; but alas! within less than forty days I began to
> question all again.[24]

By now he was reading the Bible from cover to cover and finding Paul's letters "sweet and pleasant". The Bible was precious to him. All its words were of equal authority and he might gain comfort anywhere. In Luke's version of the Parable of the Great Feast, he felt that the words "And yet there is roome" had been spoken by the Lord thinking of him.[25] The aged John Wesley broke down at this point in a sermon on the Great Feast, while my own mother believed that Christ prayed for her in John 17 when he interceded for believers in the future.

In line with a great tradition Bunyan allegorised obscure passages which seemed to refer to regulations of a past culture. The clean and unclean beasts of Deuteronomy 14 were types of men.[26]

But Scripture often spoke condemnation and disturbed his peace. It is

21

significant that again and again he not only reads words, but hears a voice. And sometimes the voice raises questions and casts doubts. Calvinist theology interprets for him the Scriptures. And he wonders if he is of the elect, or if for him the day of grace is past. He longs to be called by Christ. Were not the commands "Follow me!" "Come after me!" for him? And then he is made sick when he reads of Christ in Mark: He went up into a mountain, *and called to him whom he would* and they came unto him." Suppose Christ had no liking for him, will not choose him!

There were struggles still with the temptations of a passionate nature. He encountered the Ranters, antinomians, who had perverted the friend who had first introduced him to Bible reading. His lusty, carnal nature, "a young man in his prime", was attracted to the dispensation from sexual morality, but he seems to have resisted without undue struggle. Whatever a Freud might say, sexual temptations were not uppermost for Bunyan. But although he had ceased outwardly to curse and to blaspheme, within he was prone to the most terrible thoughts of evil. When he was admitted to fellowship in the Bedford church he found the Lord's Supper and Christ's command for its continuance very precious: "for by it the Lord did come down upon my conscience with the discovery of his death for my sins, and, as I then felt, did as if he plunged me in the vertue of the same". The exaltation did not last and soon the sacrament became a means of the vilest temptations to blasphemy "and to wish some deadly thing to those that then did eat thereof". As so often, he had recourse to prayer. He "bent" himself to pray to be kept from such temptations, "and also to cry to God to bless the Bread and Cup to them as it went from mouth to mouth". After nine months the power of the dominical command reasserted itself and he was able to discern the Lord's Body "as broken for (his) sins".[27]

Earlier he had been assailed by doubts, revived in our day, as to the finality of Christ. Were the Scriptures true? Were they not "cunningly devised fables"? Was there a God, a Christ? Were not Islamic Scriptures as good as the Christian? Why should we alone in one corner of the earth be blessed with the knowledge of the way to heaven, "if there were indeed a heaven"? "Everyone doth think his own religion rightest, both Jews and Moors and Pagans; and how if all our Faith and Christ and Scripture should be but a think-so too?"[28]

The force of these thoughts sometimes made him curse God. His despair was because he felt that those who really loved God could not entertain such thoughts. But far worse was the temptation that arose from his fear that he might have committed the unpardonable sin, the sin against the

Holy Spirit. And not only so, the tempter provoked him "to desire to sin that sin".

He was not capable of receiving much external aid. In the earlier time of his torments he

> could attend upon none of the Ordinances of God but with sore and great affliction; yea then I was most distressed with blasphemies: if I have been hearing the Word, the uncleanness, blasphemies, and despair, would hold me as Captive there; if I have been reading then sometimes I had sudden thoughts to question all I read; sometimes again my mind would be so strangely snatched away, and possessed with other things, that I have neither known, nor regarded, nor remembered so much as the sentence that but now I have read.[29]

John Gifford, minister of the Independent congregation at Bedford, a fine pastor, talked to him and invited him to a group in his house, which met, rather like the Methodist class-meetings of the next century, to confer "about the dealings of God with the soul". This seemed but to expose the wickedness of his heart, increase his temptations and diminish his longing for God. When he told the people of God of his condition they pitied him and reminded him of the promises:

> but they had as good have told me that I must reach the sun with my finger, as have bidden me receive or relie upon the Promise, and as soon as I should have done it, all my sence and feeling was against me, and I saw I had a heart that would sin, and lay under a Law that would condemn.[30]

The need to refute the Quakers strengthened his faith for they seemed to deny the historical faith of Christianity and half the creeds in their contention for the light within. They drove Bunyan to Scripture to ratify the objective atonement he needed.[31]

Sometimes Christians made no attempt to comfort him. He once took an opportunity to "break (his) mind" to "an Antient Christian" and confided in him among other things that he feared he had sinned against the Holy Ghost. He "told me, *He thought so too*". Further conversation showed that this good man was "a stranger to much combat with the Devil". So Bunyan could rely on no one but God, though he, it seems, spoke with two voices.[32]

He did, however, find help from one quarter. He had a great desire to study the experience of someone in the past, for he felt that such a person might have plumbed the depths, whereas people of his own time, as one so often feels about one's contemporaries, were shouting from the shallow end. It so happened that there fell into his hands an old, battered copy of Martin Luther's commentary on Galatians. (Was Bunyan aware that Luther had died little more than a hundred years before? He writes as though he were one of the early Fathers, though perhaps in those days time passed more slowly and seemed longer.)

In Luther he found a kindred spirit. After Tyndale and the early Reformers, Luther had not exercised an influence on English Protestantism comparable with that of Calvin and the Swiss. Bunyan was not concerned with Luther's sacramental and political theology, both of which the majority of English divines deplored.[33] He may not have been aware of them. But Luther's experience was similar to that of Bunyan in his psychological traumas and his struggles for an assurance which no external aids could bring, not the sacramental system of the Church nor the counsels of his saintly confessor. Gordon Rupp wrote a life of the young Luther in terms of *The Pilgrim's Progress*, which he called *Luther's Progress to the Diet of Worms* and the chapter headings follow Christian's course. Reading 'Luther on Galatians, Bunyan "found (his) condition in (Luther's) experience, so largely and profoundly handled, as if his Book had been written out of my heart".[34] Luther's temptations were his, "Blasphemy, Desperation and the like", and he discovered from Luther that "the law of Moses, as well as the Devil, Death, and Hell, hath a very great hand therein". He testifies: "I do prefer this book of Mr Luther upon the Galathians (excepting the Holy Bible) before all the books that ever I have seen, as most fit for a wounded Conscience."[35]

This was, perhaps, the end of the beginning of Bunyan's struggles, but the worst temptation was to come, not unrelated to the world of trade, of "getting and spending", the market economy, which was all about him; "and that was to sell and part with this most blessed Christ, to exchange him for the things of this life". This lasted for a year. Scripture once more was ambivalent. Bunyan found comfort in the promise of Leviticus: "For the land shall not be sold for ever, for the land is mine, saith God" (Lev. 25:23). But in every act of his life, the most homely and basic, the inward voice would say "Sell Christ for this, or sell Christ for that; sell him, sell him." And another passage of Scripture came to haunt him for months on end: "or profane person, as Esau, who for one morsel of meat sold his birthright. For ye know how that afterward, when he would have inherited the blessing, he was rejected: for he found no place of repentance, though he sought it carefully with tears" (Hebrews 12:16–17).

Everything coalesced here, the temptation to sell Christ for worldly ease, pleasure and advantage, the danger of final rejection through the inability to repent, itself perhaps a sign that the unforgivable sin against the Spirit had been committed.

Bunyan shows tremendous powers of reasoning, adducing one text against another, engaged in dialectic, but mostly in Doubting Castle with occasional paroles, as some word of promise broke for a while the chains of his captivity. And beneath all was still the terrible sense that he half-wanted to sin against the Spirit.

He compares himself with the great sinners of the Bible, especially David the adulterer and murderer, Peter who denied Christ, Judas who really did sell him. Two of them were forgiven. But David's sins were against the law of Moses, his against the law of Christ; Peter, to whom he felt closest, had denied his Master, he had sold his Saviour. Yet was he quite a Judas? He had not sinned deliberately, rather against his strivings and his prayers.[36]

Most of the time he was near despair. And he was not helped by reading Nathaniel Bacon, *A Relation of the Fearful Estate of Francis Spira in the year 1548*. This was as salt in fresh wounds:

> Every sentence in that book, every groan of that man, with all the rest
> of his actions in his dolors, as his tears, his prayers, his gnashing of
> teeth, his wringing of hands, his twining and twisting, languishing and
> pining away under that mighty hand of God that was upon him, was
> as knives and daggers in my Soul.[37]

There were physical symptoms, trembling and shaking, stomach discomforts, and a feeling that his breast bone would split asunder. He thought of Judas whose bowels gushed out.[38] There was no lasting peace from the thought of the merits of his redeemer. He was worse than any notorious sinner of the Old Testament. Blood-stained as they were, they had not parted with Christ. They had not sold their Saviour.

There were days of remission under the promises; but not for long. He was even tempted to think that prayer was not for him; yet in one flash of illumination, albeit temporary, he thought to himself, "I can but die; and if it be so, it shall once be said, That such a one died at the foot of Christ in Prayer." But the words about Esau supervened.

On and on it went, the oscillation between momentary comfort and almost total despair. Scripture mostly tortured him, but the promises were not wholly obliterated. And one morning when he was fearfully at prayer, there darted upon him the text "My grace is sufficient". This with Esau "would be like a pair of scales within my mind, sometimes one end would be uppermost, and sometimes again the other".[39]

In the end he came to see that the "Word of the law and Wrath must give place to the Word of Life and Grace; because, though the Word of Condemnation be glorious, yet the Word of life and salvation, doth far exceed in Glory".[40] Had Luther triumphed in the end? Was the seed sown from Bunyan's reading of the preface to Galatians that all Scripture is not of equal authority, as the Calvinist Puritans believed, but that the word of Grace annuls the word of Law?

Esau was not finally defeated nor did Bunyan's temptations cease. As we have seen, he was much assailed at Communion after his reception into the Church. And while, as a preacher, he had much freedom in the pulpit, even as he descended the steps he fell again into the old doubts and temptations. But Grace began to prevail. He found supreme comfort in Joshua 20 – a word of grace through allegory from the Old Testament, which for him remained just as much a book about Christ as the New: "And if the avenger of blood pursue the slayer, then they that are the elders of the city of refuge, shall not deliver him into his hand, because he smote his neighbour unwittingly and hated him not aforetime." Who today would read those words as anything other than an example of humane ancient justice? Bunyan felt that they applied to him, for his sins had been unwitting and he had not hated Christ his neighbour though he had sinned against him; he had prayed to him and fought against temptation. So he had a right to enter the city after all. The apostles, the elders, however severe their judgements against sin, were not to deliver him up.

There remained the awesome question of the unforgivable sin. Those who commit it are assuredly shut out, for them there is no more sacrifice for sins, they are denied a share in the promise of life in this world or the next, and they are excluded from Christ's intercession, for he will not own them. Yet, much comforted by the supremacy of the words of Grace, Bunyan began to look again at the more terrible Scriptures. Hebrews was the most severe of the writings, with its denial of second repentance to apostates and its severity against wilful sin. But now Bunyan began to feel that he had not sinned under these categories after all. And as for Esau, here again he brought Scripture to bear on Scripture and convinced himself that Esau's great sin was in despising his birthright, which is the analogy of Christian regeneration. Thus he lost the blessing which for the Christian is eternal life. And he found no place of repentance because his tears were not for loss of the birthright, which he continued to despise, but for the loss of the blessing. Thus Bunyan did not fall under Esau's condemnation.

He now read the Bible with new eyes as the book predominantly of Grace. But his conscience remained bruised and tender until one day in the field another sentence fell upon his soul, "Thy righteousness is in heaven." His righteousness did not depend upon his own moods, nor even upon his feelings towards goodness and evil, but on the exalted Saviour, "Jesus Christ, the same, yesterday, today and for ever". His own righteousness, Christ, was ever before the throne of God.

Christ was now his all, "all my Wisdom, all my Righteousness, all my Sanctification, and all my Redemption". He need not worry about the coins in his pocket, for his gold, Christ, was safe in his trunk at home.

"Further, the Lord did also lead me into the mystery of Union with this Son of God, that I was joyned to him, that I was flesh of his flesh, and bone of his bone, and now that was a sweet word to me, Ephesians 5:30.[41] This is not the union of the contemplative, the mystery into which the mystic enters. It is the union which is the "focal theme" of Calvinist spirituality; the union which comes through faith, which is complementary to the love of God in the Catholic tradition. This union marks the beginning of the Christian life, what Bunyan's contemporary, the ejected Presbyterian minister Walter Marshall, closely following Calvin, called "the first work of saving grace in our hearts".[42] Yet it is described in Scripture in metaphors of the utmost intimacy, as those Bunyan cites from Ephesians. There is the Fourth Gospel's Bread and eater, Vine and branches. Marshall would even dare to find an analogy in the hypostatic union of the Father and the Son in the mystery of the Godhead. But this spirituality would hesitate to use the language of deification in spite of the safeguards in eastern Orthodox teaching, that, for instance, we may share the energies not the essence of God. The distinction between creature and creator is always maintained. And the union never ignores the Church, the godly fellowship of God's chosen people who, though saved individually through an intensity of personal conflict, travel together and reach the heaven which is a celestial city, a glorified society of the saints.

Bunyan analyses the causes of the temptations he endured and their eventual benefits.

He felt that he had failed in prayer, in that he prayed for the removal of present troubles and for fresh discoveries of love in Christ; but not to be kept from evil to come. And he thought that he had tempted God like Gideon putting out a fleece when he should have "believed and ventured upon (God's) word" and trusted the all-seeing eye of him who can discern the secret thoughts of the heart.

He claimed many advantages from all his afflictions, perhaps above all the conviction that "great sins do draw out great grace". Without his temptations he would not have known the heights and depths of mercy. He might, had the hymn been written then, have sung with Charles Wesley, in spite of the latter's Arminianism, this interpretation of Ephesians 3:17–18:

> My trespass was grown up to heaven;
>   But far above the skies,
> In Christ abundantly forgive,
>   I see thy mercies rise.
>
> The depth of all redeeming love
>   What angel tongue can tell?
> O may I to the utmost prove
>   The gift unspeakable.
>
> Deeper than hell it plucked me thence;
>   Deeper than inbred sin,
> Jesus's love my heart shall cleanse
>   When Jesus enters in.

The Scriptures became the keys of the kingdom of heaven to him. They proclaimed the goodness and severity of God, breaking him to pieces alike with the glory of the holiness of God and the compassion of Christ. He was made to turn over every leaf of the Bible "with much diligence mixed with trembling". And he learned, though with much agony, not to put by the word of promise when it came into his mind, but to lean his weary soul on it that he might-not sink for ever into what he was later to describe as the Slough of Despond. He came to rest on the Johannine text: "And him that comes to me I will in no wise cast out."

He goes on to tell of other temptations and sicknesses. In physical weakness temptations seemed to gather force, but they were now refuted by the paramount word of Grace. Once in a depression allied to physical ills, there suddenly sounded in his heart as he sat musing by the fire the words "I must go to Jesus" Neither he nor his wife could tell where in Scripture these might be found, but "I had not sat above two or three minutes when there came bolting in upon me, And to an innumerable company of angels, and withal, Hebrews the twelfth about Mount Zion was set before mine eyes."

And so the account of Bunyan's conflicts in *Grace Abounding* ends. He has attained a certain stability though not the full assurance that might make him arrogant or priggish like some who have been converted, such as, later, John Wesley in the days immediately after his experience in Aldersgate on 24th May 1738. (Wesley soon mellowed). Had he been changed by a lightning flash or one all-commanding voice, instead of many, often in conflict, he would not have become the humble, compassionate, tender-hearted pastor that he was. "Bowels becometh pilgrims", in Christiana's words. He would certainly not have been the author of *The Pilgrim's Progress* for this is *Grace Abounding* writ large. Christian with his burden is Bunyan and the progress is not an ascent to heaven as by a chariot of fire and a whirlwind, but a lone trail with constant hazards, Vanity Fair, much conflict, Apollyon to contend with and a dark valley. There is a church with evangelist, the Interpreter, the House Beautiful, the shepherds on the Delectable Mountains; there are companions, Faithful, the martyr, and Hopeful, bringer of good cheer; but, like Bunyan, Christian's journey is a deeply personal odyssey and he almost sinks in the river at the last.

We may wonder why Bunyan had to undergo such inward tortures and we may curse religion, as he did at times, and want to hurl the Bible out of the window. Why should people be subject to such psychological torments because they believe that they live in the presence of a God who can save them or damn them in an eternity which is not proven and may be a chimera of diseased and fearful imaginations? And why should they believe that the key of understanding is contained in some ancient texts from a distant and primitive world, which deal in the concepts of a pre-scientific age and a flat earth?

One thing must be clear. The form of Bunyan's pathology may have been created by the Bible and the traditional Christian scheme, but had not his anxieties been so cast, they would still have been there. Because they may be free of religion and sacred writings, people are not necessarily free from anxieties or less prone to breakdowns. They may no longer have a book in their hand but they still stand beneath the walls of the City of Destruction with a burden on their backs and cry "What shall we do?"

Bunyan was fortunate because in spite of the grim and bloody episodes of Scripture, its horrific realism about the things that people can do, even in the name of their God, it is a story which ends in suffering love, and its governing theme, as Bunyan came at last to discover, is of a strength made perfect in weakness, and the Crucified risen from the dead.

It may be that Bunyan's later bold witness to the world, his contentions and suffering – in secular terms, for freedom of speech and human rights – were the result of his inner struggles. His courage came from his fighting within and his battles with fear. And although he travelled an often solitary way, he found his company among the lowly humble. They brought him joy and saved him from complacency and the self-satisfactions of respectability and the keeping of the Commandments. They showed him that there was more to Christianity than the good conscience of a dutiful squire, or the seemly genuflections of a bejewelled communicant.

3
Preacher and Controversialist

Bunyan became a member of the Bedford Separatist Congregation in 1655. After a year or so members of the church recognised in him a potential gift of preaching and he was invited to deliver "a word of exhortation" at their meetings. He did this twice and the members were both "affected and comforted", so that he proceeded to the next stage, which was to accompany one or two of them on expeditions to villages outside Bedford, where, again, his address would be to members only. Once more he was well received. In consequence, "after some solemn prayer to the Lord with fasting", he was called and appointed to the public ministry of the Word, not only to the congregation of the committed, but to those far and wide who were not believers and to whom he felt a special vocation or, as he says, "a secret pricking forward thereto".[1] By August 1657 this work led to him being absent so frequently from his own congregation that he was not able to serve as a deacon.

It is clear that he began to preach while still "most sorely afflicted with the fiery darts of the evil one concerning (his) eternal state".[2] He may be deemed one to whom the later words of the Moravian Peter Böhler to John Wesley might apply, "Preach faith till you have it." He was aware of some talent of speech, some gift of words, which he must not bury in the ground, even though he was assailed by self-doubt and lacking in assurance. He needed the authorisation of his fellow church-members, which their rules required. It is obvious too that he was constrained by "tenderness", his interest in people and his desire that however uncertain his own grasp of faith or assurance of salvation they should not be denied the message of the gospel. And God had given him "some measure of bowels" to try to find the Word and the words to awaken the consciences of the depraved and the indifferent. There is no doubt that he was, in the cliché of our time, "an effective communicator", with the charisma of the evangelist, but he did not prevail by technique or practised skill; rather

31

because he spoke from his own heart and his own experience. "I preached what I felt, what I smartingly did feel."[3]

But this at first was:

even that under which my poor Soul did groan and tremble to astonishment . . . indeed I have been as one sent to them from the dead. I went myself in chains to preach to them in chains and carried the fire in my own conscience that I perswaded them to beware of.

He entered the pulpit in fear, found tremendous liberty as he preached and then descended into the dungeon of Giant Despair once more.

Bunyan was primarily a preacher. His theological works had their genesis in his sermons. They are in fact extended sermons. And the activity of preaching was his pilgrim's progress. Within two years he had entered into greater peace with God and stability of faith. He began to preach less of sin and more of Christ; Christ in his "offices", that is, in the whole range of what he could do for the human soul and for the world; Christ as the saving alternative to the bogus securities of getting and spending or of the philosophies of godless self-interest. And in consequence of this, "God led me into something of the mystery of union with Christ" and this he came to preach also, the union, which, as we have seen, was the heart of Calvinist spirituality.

The preaching

In his brilliant pioneer work, *John Bunyan: mechanick preacher* (1934), William York Tindall showed that Bunyan was by no means unique. There were many other contemporary preachers among those who worked with their hands, who earned their daily bread with pots and pans and domestic repairs, cobblers and tailors. This period of English history was remarkable for a great outburst of preaching, not confined to the pulpits and the liturgy nor to those able to quote authorities and adorn their discourses with tags from the classics and citations from Scripture in "the languages of the Holy Ghost". "Great was the company of preachers" and they propagated their doctrines often in conflict with each other and the established order and, so governments were prone to fear, to the undermining of society.

They were heirs to a tradition as old as their faith itself, which was indistinguishable from it. Christianity was born in preaching, in the tradition of the Hebrew prophets. There were the stories told by Jesus and the stories told about him, the parables, the *kerygma*, the exposition of apostolic writings. The gospel originated in the ages of rhetoric, when "all culture, all the education of antiquity, tended more and more . . . towards this one ideal, the orator's ideal, the ideal of good speaking".[4]

There was rhetoric of a kind, though not of the schools, in the preaching of medieval friars and seventeenth-century mechanics. They learned their art, rough as it may have been, from one another. They listened to their fathers and fellows and were soaked in the style of popular proclamation, with vivid, homely images and metaphors. They may not have read much theology, but if they had the sensitivity which is part of the genius of preaching they would breathe in the breezes of the intellectual climate and impart its ethos as truly as if they had spent hours in libraries.

The fact that the gospel was proclamation rather than philosophy has affected its influence until our own time. Not that Christianity has lacked philosophers from early years, or that the kerygmatic and the prophetic are inimical to rational thought. "Come let us reason together (argue this out), says the Lord" (Isa. 1:18). The preacher seeks to persuade, but to capture more than the mind, to obtain, in Newman's terminology, "real" rather than "notional" assent. (And Bunyan attacks "notionists", "wordy professors", that is, those who claim to be Christians and go through the motions of Christianity in speech and action without being "born again", who have the word but not the power of the gospel.) The preacher would sway the emotions, direct the will. He makes offers and demands. The words quoted from Isaiah are followed not by a philosophic argument but by a promise, "though your sins are scarlet, they may yet be white as snow; though they are dyed crimson, they may become white as wool". And there may equally be denunciation of the evils of the age and of individual sins and errors, together with the requirements of God, justice, mercy and humility. The preacher may use dialectic but must beware over-many qualifications which destroy the message. Nor may he be too speculative. Although he hopes for great freedom of expression that he may range far and wide in the universe of the divine Grace and in the fields of attentive and eager minds, he is constrained by the faith he proclaims. Rival forms of Christianity may regard him as a heretic, but he must not betray his fellow-believers. He must come to a conclusion and expect one from the hearers. To achieve this the preaching must capture the imagination. It cannot deal in great ideas, in lofty concepts, alone.

In the first part of *The Pilgrim's Progress* there is a picture of the preacher shown to Christian in the Interpreter's House. It is:

33

of a very grave Person . . . and this was the fashion of it. It had eyes lift up to heaven, the best of Books in its hand, the Law of Truth was written upon its lips, the World was behind its back; it stood as if it pleaded with Men and a Crown of Gold did hang over its head.[5]

The Interpreter explains, in New Testament metaphors, that this man begets (spiritual) children, travails in bringing them to birth, and then is their nurse. His posture and his biblical resource and the truth written upon his lips make plain "that his work is to know and unfold dark things to sinners". He opens the divine secrets of mercy and judgement. And he must do this from a renunciation of this world and a belief that his reward is in the world to come, for here he may well receive obloquy, scorn and persecution, as Bunyan and many others did under the Stuarts. The preacher is the divinely authorised spiritual guide. Not always does he counsel by public proclamation. He may talk to groups or one to one. But it is he, rather than the sacerdotal priest, who leads the pilgrims in the right way, mediating the divine mercy, resolving cases of conscience, speaking always of God and the glory to be revealed. This was what preaching meant – and not only to Puritans – in the seventeenth century.[6] Since then we have become tired of words and suspicious of rhetoric. We have wanted to work things out for ourselves and have had less faith in those with presumed special gifts, qualifications and knowledge, even if it be experiential. We may feel that we learn more from one another in group discussion than from experts in the pulpit or on the dais. In any case the experts may differ in theology, biblical interpretation and moral judgement and the pulpit may be a tower of Babel. But in times of crisis the Word may become paramount again and we long for prophets, those who can declare the counsels of God, justify his ways and guide us through "this maddening maze of things".

There was an influential Puritan divine, John Owen (1616–83), who became an Independent in churchmanship in his twenties and was their most considerable seventeenth-century theologian, one of the founding fathers of English Congregationalism. He was Dean of Christ Church and Vice Chancellor of Oxford University under Cromwell, where he formed a gathered Church and scandalised some by sartorial vanities including powdered hair and a cocked hat. A Nonconformist after 1662, he became one of Bunyan's friends in London, and is said to have told Charles II that he would sacrifice all his learning to preach like the tinker.[7]

Like all Puritan preaching, Bunyan's was rooted deeply in Scripture. He asserted that his Bible and his Concordance were his only library.[8] The whole of the Bible was the infallible word of God. John Owen declared that every tittle and iota of Scripture was from God, dictated by God.[9] God spoke three languages, Hebrew, Chaldean and Greek, which left a problem of translation! Bunyan was deemed at a disadvantage by learned expositors because he had not the original tongues. He boasted of his ignorance, sarcastically pointing out, in a manner almost worthy of Lloyd George, that Pontius Pilate could speak Hebrew, Greek and Latin.[10] His friends felt that he won an argument with a taunting scholar on this issue:

> Then said Mr Bunyan, Have you the original? Yes, said the scholar. Nay, but, said Mr Bunyan, have you the very self-same original copies that were written by the penmen of the scriptures, prophets and apostles? No, said the scholar, but we have the true copies of those originals. How do you know that? said Mr Bunyan. How? said the scholar. Why, we believe what we have is a true copy of the original. Then, said Mr Bunyan, so I do believe our English Bible is a true copy of the original. Then away rid the scholar.[11]

It is not certain what translation into English Bunyan used, though there is every likelihood that it was, in his early days, the Geneva Bible, with its rendering "breeches" in Genesis 3:7 and its marginal comments, approved by Calvinists. Later he seems to have adopted the Authorised Version, by then less distrusted by Puritans.[12]

Bunyan is adamant that Scripture is necessary both to self-knowledge and the knowledge of God, without both of which one cannot be saved.[13] In his earliest sermon, *A Few Sighs from Hell*, he is aware that there are many, like himself at first, for whom the Bible simply did not come alive. He makes the indifferent soul say:

> The Scriptures, thought I, what are they? a dead letter, a little ink and paper, of three or four shillings price. Alas, what is Scripture, give me a Ballad, a Newsbook, *George* on horseback, or *Bevis* of Southampton . . . but for the holy Scriptures I cared not. But there is no alternative. The soul will remain in darkness until the Scriptures speak with the voice of God. Then the converted will live in the Bible. The word will be his rule.[14]

Not that Scripture is all comfort, as Bunyan so well knew, but what he had learned from his own struggles, doubtless with the help of John Gifford and the Bedford Congregation, was not to let those isolated texts which had alternately brought him comfort and despair stand by themselves, but to compare Scripture with Scripture and relate all to the totality of God's saving work. He came to interpret Scripture not only by itself but by the theology which the Puritans believed they derived from it.

He inherited the medieval hermeneutic of fourfold meanings in Scripture, though the Puritans felt that these were applications of one authoritative sense. But his poetic imagination made him a natural allegorist, however saving or damning he believed this plain, literal sense to be. He came to argue, since he did not know Jülicher, that the parables of Jesus were the justification of allegory in the interpretation of Scripture.[15] This could be very powerful, as in *The Holy City*, a work of 1665 in his imprisonment. It is a meditation on Revelation 21 and 22. He may not be far from the spirit and method of Scripture itself in seeing the New Jerusalem as the fulfilment of prophecies, such as Jeremiah 31:10–12, in which the scattered flock of Israel is brought to sing "in the height of Zion". John R. Knott, jun. has commented:

> Bunyan's insistent allegorizing of the detail of the New Jerusalem, with its walls and gates and jewels, may strain the patience of a modern reader, yet it is hard not to respond to his striking vision of the recovery of the purity of apostolic doctrine and the unity of the primitive church through the agency of the Word. When Antichrist falls, and the Gospel "breaks out in its primitive glory", Bunyan insists, "all shall be recovered and brought into order again by the golden reed of the word of God".[16]

This was a feature of Bunyan's preaching throughout his career. The last of his works to be published in his lifetime is *Solomon's Temple Spiritualised* (1688). The title itself betrays allegory. "See therefore the mystery of God in these things." The most intriguing example is Bunyan's seeing in the "network" of the capitals of the temple pillars a type of the net of the gospel by which the apostles caught their converts.

Allegory has not been encouraged in preachers of recent decades or in modern theology. It is deemed remote from our thought-forms and generally dubious. It is hardly compatible with historical criticism of the Scriptures and may appear dishonest in seeking to wrest an interpretation congenial to its practitioner or evade the plain, literal meaning, which may be too disturbing for comfort. A notorious instance is the allegory of the "two swords" of Luke 22:38 to represent the Pope's spiritual power and the Emperor's temporal. It has its fascination. I shall never forget the interest of a class, admittedly of mature students, when I read them Augustine's allegorisation of the parable of the Good Samaritan. Eyes lit up and pencils were busier than usual. And Andrew Louth has powerfully advocated a "return to allegory". He invokes Hans-Georg Gadamer and T. S. Eliot in castigating the romantic notion of the "original meaning" of any text. "Understanding is the result of genuine engagement: it is less a result with an objective content than an event in the life of the one seeking to understand." And allegory, used with the careful distinctions of a writer such as the modern French Catholic Henri de Lubac, helps us to participate in the mystery of Christ. It is not definitive. It does not prove anything. But it is "a way of making a synthetic vision out of the images and events of the biblical narrative". It helps us to discern the pattern of the divine love which is shaped through all the strange, confused and terrible events of Scripture and its characters deformed by sin and restored by grace.[17]

So Bunyan's power as a preacher came not only from his living in Scripture interpreted as a result of his struggles and his winning through to humble confidence, but from the vividness of his imagination. Puritan preaching had been "plain and perspicuous" in contrast to that of Anglicans such as Lancelot Andrewes and John Donne. It avoided their literary conceits and playing with words. It was neither "witty" nor "metaphysical", that is, it neither sought to sparkle by mental agility and fine metaphors nor to display learning by far-fetched imagery (though this was always employed to illustrate the mystery of Christ and the Church). Puritan preaching was based on the prescriptions of William Perkins in *The Arte of Prophecying*, first published in Latin in 1592 and in English in 1607. Perkins maintains that two things are required in preaching, "the hiding of humane wisdom, and the demonstration or showing of the spirit". The application should be "to the life and manners of men in a *simple and plaine speech*".[18] This Puritan preaching in spite of itself was not without eloquence and power. It "held" audiences in the universities, as well as in the common way. It dealt with those matters on which it was believed the eternal destinies of its hearers hung. What is dried sea-weed to our time was living water to many in the decades after the Reformation. But it did not deal in the refinements of academic sophistry; it offered what John Wesley was to call "the old, coarse Gospel".

The disparagement and wilful concealment of learning opened the gate to the "mechanicks" during the civil wars and the Commonwealth. After the Restoration there was a most interesting change. As Roger Pooley has written, "The terms of the argument between Puritans and Laudians in the 1630s (plainness versus ostentation) are almost exactly reversed in the 1660s and 1670s when it is the new Anglicans who emphasize plainness against what they see as Puritan and nonconformist excess."[19] The Latitude men, the moralists, the practical preachers were gaining ground in the English Church. To them the Puritans seemed scholastics, dilating on justification by faith alone, with its dangers of antinomianism, agonising over their election, whipping up emotion with their intensity and warnings, making Christianity mysterious whereas it was a straightforward way of life, sanctified common sense, "the republication of natural religion", "the conservation of socially-recognised values". This way was to be chosen freely, as Bishop Butler was to say, "in a cool hour", not in a frantic "fleeing from the wrath to come" in the hope of gaining assurance that you were one of the few to be saved.

As is already clear from his use of allegory, Bunyan was not a "plain" preacher in the new Anglican sense. By the end of his life he may have seemed old-fashioned, preaching in a style no longer in vogue, in an idiom as out-dated as that of John Henry Newman or Alexander Whyte addressing their hearers in the second person singular in contrast to a late-twentieth-century broadcast homily. But he was folksy and colloquial as he confronted his hearers with the issues of life and death, heaven and hell. And he had the gift of filling out the brief stories and sparse records of Scripture with human detail. Their brevity demands imaginative enlargement. That is basic to the technique of meditation, so prevalent in the post-Reformation era, not least in the *Spiritual Exercises* of Ignatius Loyola, founder of the Jesuits. Its perennial danger is that hearers may mistake the play of fancy for recorded fact. In the early published sermon, *A Few Sighs from Hell*, Bunyan imagines the wealthy Dives refusing to admit the beggar Lazarus to his table: "What, shall I regard *Lazarus*? Scrubbed, beggarly *Lazarus*? What, shall I so far dishonour my fair, sumptuous and gay house, with such a scabbed creep-hedge as he: no, I scorne he should be entertained under my roof."[20]

In a work of 1684 we find the same imaginative vividness in an account of the death of John the Baptist, though this was no artistic self-indulgence nor desire to entertain: he was describing the sufferings of the faithful at the end of Charles II's reign when, after the failed attempt to exclude the Roman Catholic James from the throne, persecution had returned at its fiercest:

> The executioner comes to John; now, whether he was at dinner, or asleep, or whatever he was about, the bloody man bolts in upon him, and the first word he salutes him with is, Sir, strip, lay down your neck, for I am come to take away your head. But hold, stay;

wherefore? pray, let me commit my soul to God. No, I must not stay; I am in haste: slap, says his sword, and off falls the good man's head.[21]

The outstanding example of Bunyan's inventiveness in the imaginative enlargement of Scripture is in one of his most popular sermons, *Come and Welcome to Jesus Christ* (1678). This is tenderly evangelical on the text "All that the Father giveth me shall come to me; and him that cometh to me I will in no wise cast out" (John 6:37). The Calvinist doctrine of predestination which the first part of the verse seems to support is transcended by the warmth and emotion with which Bunyan expounds the second part. Like a medieval preacher he turns the words "shall come" into a character of that name. "Why, *Shall-come* answered all this . . . *Shall come, can raise them from this Death.*" But when he re-tells the story of the Prodigal Son, he fills out the economical details of St Luke by imagining the Prodigal's state of mind. The fact that the Father greeted him with a kiss must have meant that he needed reassurance, the removing of doubts and fears, for which kisses are often used in Scripture. And so Bunyan recounts the fluctuations of the Prodigal's mood on his journey home from the far country. He starts off in confidence, but *en route* he has

> many a thought, both this way and that; as whether his Father would receive him, or no? As thus: I said, *I would go to my Father*: but, if when I come at him, he should ask me, *Where I have all this while bin*; What must I say then? Also, if he asks me, *What is become of the portion of Goods he gave me*. What shall I say then? If he asks me, *Who have been my companions*; What shall I say then?

No wonder the Prodigal would need a kiss from his Father before all else! The truly awakened soul is prone (like Bunyan himself) "to give way . . . to despondings and heart-misgivings; no marvel if he did sink in his mind between the time of his first setting-out, and that of his coming to the Father". Bunyan had some misgivings about this "inventing". In *Come and Welcome to Jesus Christ* he suggests that this heightened imagination may be the reason why the returning sinner is brought so near to despair. He himself is using for the purposes of conversion the very faculty of the mind that causes so much woe. He had expressed some questionings about it in *A Few Sighs from Hell*. In the margin of his lavish re-telling of the story of Dives and Lazarus he asks how the preacher can possibly know what went on in hell or how to fill out the places where Christ is silent. And he answers, "This language is sometimes heard at the gallows, but for ought I can learn, it is more to be heard in hell." He is aware that there is ambivalence in the use of the imagination. It can be for good or ill, hope or despair, truth or vain fancy.[22]

In a late work, *Good News for the Vilest of Men or The Jerusalem Sinner Saved,* there is an instance of Bunyan's oratorical style, when he catalogues the iniquities of Despair:

> *Despair*! when we have a God of Mercy, and a Redeeming Christ *Alive*! For shame forbear: let them despair that dwell where there is no God, and that are confined to those Chambers of Death, which can be reached by no Redemption.
>
> A Living Man despair! When he is *chid* for murmuring and complaining! Oh! so long as we are where Promises *swarm*, where Mercy is *proclaimed* where Grace *reigns* and where *Jerusalem sinners* are privileged with the first offer of Mercy, *it is a base thing to despair*!
>
> *Despair* undervalues the Promise, undervalues the Invitation, undervalues the proffer of Grace. *Despair* undervalues the ability of God the Father, and the redeeming Blood of Christ his Son: Oh, unreasonable *Despair*!
>
> *Despair* makes Man *God's* Judge; 'tis a Controller of the Promise, a Contradicter of Christ in his large offers of Mercy: And one that undertakes to make *Unbelief* the great manager of our Reason and Judgement, in determining what God can and will do for sinners.

And so on in like vein until: *"Despair*! It drives a man to the study of his own ruine and brings him at last to be his own Executioner."[23]

Bunyan, like Luther, may always have trembled at the Word of God and felt himself driven as a leaf before it. He imparted this to his hearers, particularly when he himself was driven more by fear than love of God. In *A Few Sighs from Hell* there are lurid descriptions of the tortures of hell, which seem largely to be physical. He warns the gambler, the wanton, the spendthrift and the hypocrite:

> . . . thy soul will fall into extreme torment, and anguish as soon as ever thou dost depart this world, and there thou shalt be weeping and gnashing thy teeth, Matt. 8:11,12. *And besides all this* thou art never likely to have any ease or remedy, never look for any deliverance, if thou die out of Christ; thou shalt die in thy sins; and be tormented as many years as there are stars in the firmament, or sands on the seashore; *and besides all this*, thou must abide it for ever.[24]

In *The Resurrection of the Dead*, a work from the early years of his first imprisonment, he adheres to the belief that "when the godly think of hell it will increase their comfort".[25] This cannot simply be dismissed as sadism or masochism. It was felt to be justifiable morally on the grounds that for some fear might be the only way to salvation. It increased the preacher's intensity and passion. He must, if he could, save people from a fate of unimaginable horror, though in the attempt he had to imagine it. And it was theodicy, an assertion, however crude, of the victory of divine justice. It had no room for a sentimental view of sin. It was at least free from the Anselmian strictures against not seriously considering its gravity. Sin is incompatible with the goodness, the love and the justice of God. And there are those so sunk in it, so totally possessed by it that they are lost eternally.

Bunyan always believed this, but in his preaching grace increasingly prevailed over law. In *Good News for the Vilest of Men* he declares that austerity does not become ministers of the Gospel:

> neither in Doctrine nor in Conversation (that is, manner of life): We ourselves live by Grace: Let us give as we receive, and labour to perswade our fellow-sinners which God has left behind us, to follow after that they may partake with us of Grace. We are saved by Grace, let us live like them that are *gracious*.[26]

Earlier in the same work he declares that even those condemned at the last will recognise the sweet reasonableness of the divine justice:

> I have often thought of the day of Judgement, and how God will deal with sinners at that day: And I believe it will be managed with that sweetness, with that equitableness with that excellent Righteousness as to every sin, and circumstance, and agravation thereof, that men that are damned, before the Judgement is over, shall receive such conviction of the righteous Judgement of God upon them and of their deserts of Hell-fire, that they shall in themselves, conclude that there is all the reason in the world that they should be shut out of Heaven and go to Hell-fire; *These shall go away into everlasting fire* (Matt.25:46).[27]

Controversies

Bunyan's compassion shines through his preaching of divine wrath and judgement, but he made the offer of grace against a background of bitter controversy. This has always been true of evangelical preaching. The New

Testament itself is in constant engagement with error and heresy and Paul's language, for instance, is often far from temperate. John Wesley too was in many contentions, notably with Quietists and Calvinists; and his followers in the nineteenth-century years of expansion, though protagonists of perfect love, disputed in vitriol with scurrilous fly-sheets which led to secessions, over polity more than doctrine. It is a psychological truism that controversial vehemence may be the sign that the position attacked has almost gained the assent of its antagonist. And this may well be true of Bunyan in his early years, when, as we have seen, he may almost have capitulated to the arguments of some of the religious movements which competed for the allegiance of his troubled, searching mind. His polemics may have been as necessary to convince himself as others.

In those times there was no concern to be tender and tolerant towards opponents, to admit that they had some truth on their side, to look for the good in them and feel that consensus and not confrontation was the Christian way. These arguments were matters of life or death, heaven and hell. A false belief might lead to everlasting burnings. One could not therefore be charitable or respect an opponent's sincerity, when it was thought to rest upon a soul-destroying lie.

Bunyan's first work, *Some Gospel Truths Opened*, was published in 1656 before there was a truce to his struggles, and earlier than his public preaching, and was an attack on the Quakers. There were many reasons why at this stage Bunyan should fear the Quakers. They were making converts in Bedfordshire for they too preached the gospel to the poor, but they seemed irresponsible and eccentric enthusiasts, going naked for a sign, disrupting acts of worship, whose agitations might lead to social chaos worse than the tyranny of kings. To Bunyan they were akin to the Ranters, though outwardly more respectable and all the more dangerous for that for they cast a cloak over what Bunyan was convinced was a claimed Christian freedom resulting in immorality and social confusion (see p.11).

The nub of the dispute for Bunyan was that they assailed the very grounds of his faith and hope, they cut his lifeline to salvation. For the Quakers, salvation turned on the light within. In common with mystics, they applied Paul's words, "The letter killeth, the spirit giveth life," to the Bible, which some argued could not be the Word of God for it was too contradictory. Faith in objective, historical events, in a cosmic salvation wrought by the life, death and resurrection of a man of the first century and mediated in ages since by institutions with rites and shrines, was vain. It so rarely resulted in a change of life and conduct. There was no obvious distinction between those who "professed and called themselves Christians", who regularly took bread and wine in remembrance of Christ's death, and men and women of the world. They amassed money, made war, were compromised by business deals and politics.

But for Bunyan everything depended on what Scripture told him about something done once for all and in history, before he could ever respond to it, and quite apart from his own feeble motions towards grace. "While we were yet sinners Christ died for us": "*The new and false Christ is a Christ crucified within, dead within, risen again within in opposition to the Son of Mary, who was crucified without, dead without, risen againe without, and ascended in a cloud away from his Disciples into heaven without them.*"[28]

Bunyan felt that the Quakers failed to distinguish between "justification wrought by the man Christ without, and sanctification wrought by the Spirit of Christ within". He insists on the literal truth of the biblical records of Christ's life, death and resurrection and that "the very man Christ" will come again to judge the world. For Bunyan in 1656 this coming might be imminent; for Quakers, like most of the radical sects, to allegorise it, as with everything else, into the promise of inward transformation, was a travesty which denied the awesome solemnity as well as the comfort of the gospel. And in his most vivid style he enlarges and paraphrases the risen Christ's words from Luke 24:38–42, proving that he is not a spirit.

Some Gospel Truths Opened provoked an immediate riposte from the Quaker Edward Burrough in *The True Faith of the Gospel of Peace contended for in the Spirit of Meekness*. He corrected Bunyan's confusion of Quakers with Ranters, but hardly turned the other cheek and the language is vehement for one who claims to write in a "Spirit of Meekness". He is incensed with Bunyan, whom he does not regard simply as one in the pit of theological error but as "a man given up to wickedness". He refers to his "carnal sottishness", "sinful, wicked, devilish nature", as well as "his damnable doctrines and errors".[29] Burrough is in the line of the nineteenth-century Tractarians who believed that doctrinal error betokens moral delinquency. Bunyan says that Quakers are "the greatest enemies to the Christ of God without" and castigates Burrough's "railings", "bawlings", "deceit".

It has been said that "the master-texts for Bunyan's theological understanding come from Galatians, whereas the Quaker teaching of the inner light derives from a verse in John's gospel".[30] This is true and it is perhaps ironic that Burrough, though he does not share Bunyan's belief in the supreme authority of Scripture, is willing to bandy texts with him, attempting to refute him on his own ground. But although Bunyan stands in the tradition of Paul as interpreted by Luther and the Reformation and not by all modern scholars,[31] John's is not *simpliciter* the spiritual gospel as the Quakers and others have been inclined to think, for however much John may seem to revise literalist beliefs in the parousia and possibly the sacraments, for this gospel, the Word made flesh is the sole way to God and what Christ did datably in his body on the cross is the means of union between his disciples and the Father and the drawing of humankind to himself.

The doctrine of the law and grace unfolded

Bunyan's most considerable theological treatise was published in 1659. By then his worst struggles were over, though the work is clearly born out of long spiritual agonies and *Grace Abounding* will be its commentary and confirmation. His first wife had died in the previous year leaving him with four young children. Oliver Cromwell also had died in September 1658 and the nation was in some turmoil. The Commonwealth had disappointed the hopes of those who had thought that it might bring in the kingdom of God. One of the reasons was that they could not agree among themselves as to what that might mean, and the radicals, vociferous and by no means without support, were feared by the law-abiding and the rising merchant classes. The freedom of the press was already menaced and Bunyan must have wondered how much longer his preaching could continue undisturbed.

But it is theological issues which preoccupy him here. These affect political attitudes, for all ultimately depends on a person's view of the world and the meaning of life, however little this is understood or inarticulate its expressions. Bunyan's concern is with a destiny which reaches far beyond our mortal years or the circumstances of this passing age; which begins and ends in the counsels of God. And this brings a numinous quality to what may seem tedious argumentation and controversies remote from our time.

There are conflated sermons here, a tabulation of points in homiletic fashion. There is dialogue, the question and answer of objector and apologist, and there are parables and exempla; there are conversations with God, arguments with oneself before him. And Bunyan must throughout controvert two opponents, the guilty conscience of sinners and the upholders of false gospels.

The controlling text is Romans 6:14, "For ye are not under law but under grace". But the framework of the argument is the theology of the covenants. This is central to Puritanism.

Covenant theology

The idea of covenant between God and his people is scriptural, but in the late sixteenth and first half of the seventeenth century it was an idea whose time had come in western Europe. It appealed especially to the new mercantile class, for a covenant is a bargain, in some sense a business deal, which is why it emanated from the Middle East and particularly the Jews whose heroes were more often Jacobs than Samsons. In addition it has been said that covenant theology was "an ideal theological structure to bear the Puritan religiousness. It contained within it the possibility of stressing both the emotional and the rational, the subjective and the objective". It could also be a political concept opposed to the divine right of kings, requiring a contract between rulers and ruled, a contract under God the sole absolute monarch and arbiter, before whose irresistible grace and election all were equal, however much earthly distinctions were of his appointment. This was obviously congenial to those new entrepreneurs and men of property who demanded both a voice in government and the freedom of the market. [32]

There are two covenants in Scripture, the old and the new (Jeremiah 31:31ff.), in the interpretation of Reformed theologians, the covenant of Law and the covenant of Grace. The former, summarised in the Ten Commandments, says "Do this and live". Bunyan points out in *The Doctrine of the Law and Grace Unfolded* that this, though it was "delivered to Moses from the hands of Angels on Mount Sinai", was first given to Adam in paradise and was frequently transgressed from Adam to Moses. He does not expound the commandments at length but refers the reader to the famous work of "Decalogue Dod", *A Plaine and Familiar Exposition of the Ten Commandments* (1603). Dod was assisted in this work by Robert Cleaver, a "solid Text-man" of whom little else is heard. He himself is one of the most engaging of the Puritan pastors spanning the whole period from the eighth year of Elizabeth to the execution of Laud, with a gift for bringing down the mysteries of faith to the meanest intelligence and lowliest listener. His aphorisms were comforting cottagers in the next century and his peers wanted him near them at their deaths. His exposition is a vade-mecum of Puritan practical divinity, but, like William Perkins and all the others, he applies the commandments, with Christ, not only to outward acts but to inward dispositions. Evil thoughts are condemned as well as evil actions.[33]

This means that the covenant of Law has as its first use to make us aware of our sins and to bring us to penitence because the commandments are impossible for us to keep in our unregenerate state. And it is here that we learn the wonders of the covenant of Grace, for God does not desire the death of any of his elect, though they be sinners, but rather that they turn from their wickedness and live in union with him in love. And this covenant of Grace was no divine afterthought; nor, though ratified on the cross, did it begin there. It was made between the Father and the Son before first creation. As Bunyan writes, "this covenant or Bargain was made in deed and in truth before man was in being. Oh! God thought of the salvation of man before there was any transgression of man . . . the price was agreed on before the world began . . . *the precious Blood of Christ.*" Similarly the promise of eternal life, and the choice of his saints, his people: the transaction is but secondarily with the patriarchs or with the house of Israel and Judah (Jeremiah 31:33). It does not rest on weak human will, the inconsistencies even of the saints, the contingencies of the passing ages of mankind. It is founded on the unity of the Godhead, on the eternal love of the Father and the Son; and it is perfectly fulfilled by Christ. By his obedience divine justice is satisfied and there is no pretence that sin can be overlooked or that it does not matter whether one is good or evil. "God forgives; it is his business" is sentimental and dangerous nonsense where it is not cynicism, but all the conditions of the covenant have been met by Christ and therefore I may be made right with God through union with him by faith. This identifies me with him in his death by which my sins are crucified and in his rising again by which I enter the life of God.

Bunyan tells in *The Doctrine of the Law and Grace Unfolded* – as he was to do, as we have seen, in *Grace Abounding* – of the comfort he received when that sentence fell upon his soul, "*Thy righteousness is in heaven*":

Sometimes I blesse the Lord my soul hath had the life that now I am speaking of, not only imputed to me, but the very glory of it upon my soul: For upon a time when I was under many condemnings of heart, and feared because of my sins my soul would miss of eternall glory; methought I felt in my soul such a secret motion as this, *Thy righteousness is in heaven*, together with the splendour and shining of the spirit of grace in my soul, which gave me clearly to see, that my righteousnesse by which I should be justified (from all that could condemn) was the Son of God himself, in his own person now at the right hand of his Father representing me compleat before the mercy-seat in his own self: so that I saw clearly, that night and day, where ever I was, or what ever I was a doing, still there was my righteousnesse just before the eyes of divine glory; so that the Father could never finde fault with me for any insufficiency that was in my righteousnesse, being it was compleat; neither could he say, where is it? because it was continually at his right hand.[34]

This is a difficult passage for our way of thinking. "Righteousness" seems almost a commodity, though it seems to refer to moral and spiritual qualities of personal being. It is not a term used in common speech today, though it figures much in familiar and older translations of the Bible. Ronald Knox called it "a meaningless token word".[35] Kenneth Grayston thinks that it should be abandoned as an archaism, which muffles the sound of a biblical passage "by the booming echoes of antique moralistic disputes". He understands the Greek *dikaiosyne* as primarily *God's saving goodness* and "secondarily as what makes us objects of his saving goodness, namely our *acceptability* to God".[36] This sheds some light on Bunyan. We are made acceptable to God because by faith we are incorporated into Christ, who is altogether and perfectly accepted. The High Anglican Eucharistic hymn expresses it:

> Look, Father, look on his anointed face,
> And only look on us as found in him.

There is also danger of Antinomianism in what Bunyan writes. If I lay my all on Christ and he becomes my acceptability with God, need I be concerned with my own dispositions and behaviour? Must I not leave all to him? To paraphrase the Antinomian John Saltmarsh, do I need to light my candle when I have the Sun of Righteousness?

Bunyan seems close to Antinomianism in a late work, *Questions About the Nature and Perpetuity of the Seventh-Day Sabbath*, when he says that the new law of the Spirit (Romans 8:2) is "written and preserved" in "the Heart spiritual", which, as Richard Greaves has pointed out, is not dissimilar from Saltmarsh's statement that the Holy Spirit makes the believer 'the very Law of Commandments in himself, and his heart the very two Tables of Moses", as though fulfilment of the law were automatic with entry into the covenant of Grace and the ensuing gift of the Holy Spirit. But Bunyan goes on to insist that "The whole Law as to the morality of it, is delivered into the hand of Christ, who imposes it now as a Rule of life to those that have believed in him", while in *The Doctrine of the Law and Grace Unfolded* he tells an objector that according to 1 John faith has fruits in our love for one another. There is a law for Christians and it is that of the old covenant, but not "as the old Covenant". It is rather the means whereby we express our loving response to him who has already saved us by his own blood, without our obedience to the Law. We obey now, not out of a duty we cannot perform, and a vain struggle to make ourselves good for our own satisfaction, but because God in Christ has accepted us freely and without merit and we would return love for love, love which includes our fellow human beings, as in the second great commandment of Christ.[37]

For Bunyan, whether one was under the first or second covenant was a matter of life or death – eternal life or eternal death. There is something here of the rigorism of the letter to Hebrews, to which Bunyan refers. But – and here again some would see a tendency to Antinomianism – sin almost seems a matter of indifference. However moral and virtuous you are, if you are under the law, trying to earn salvation by morality, you will be damned; if you have accepted Christ and his deliverance through a work not your own, however great your past sins and your continuing weakness and proneness to defection you will be saved. Apart from Christ and the divine grace through him there is only "a just God, a sin revenging God, a God that will by no means spare the guilty". In Christ there is infinite mercy and a love which passes knowledge and grace to cover all sin.

This seems appallingly exclusive and discouraging to "virtuous and godly living". Bunyan rules out so many whom the consensus of God-fearing humanity would regard as lights in their generation. Fidelity to scriptural commands, liberality, power in prayer, well-ordered and devout families, an inheritance in godly forebears are of no avail in themselves. Nor is "natural theology", faith in God "onely as a merciful Creator", not as of those born again into his family through Christ, who have the Spirit which is bold to cry "Abba, Father" and not simply to recite the Lord's Prayer as a decorous duty. Nor are proponents of Church order *ipso facto* among the saved. The Gospel ordinances, "as baptisme, breaking of bread, hearing, praying, meditating, or the like" may be agencies of the supreme and most tragic irony, for though they are intended to bring us close to Christ they may remove us farthest from him.

This seems indeed a narrow gate even if it leads to the large and ample paradise of God. Few, we may think, will enter it. Most will be left outside though they approach in hope and confidence. This would not worry

Bunyan since Calvinism does not expect universal salvation. Even though many are called few are chosen. But one wonders if the later Wesley may not be right after all. He was an Arminian who believed God's love in Christ was for all and abominated Calvinist election. After his evangelical conversion and in the first years of the Methodist revival, he preached the necessity of the new birth and the doctrine that one cannot be saved by works, and of the Christ who came not to call the righteous but sinners to repentance. Yet in 1767 he wrote in his journal, in an instalment published in 1771, that "a man may be saved who has no clear conceptions of it" and "a pious churchman who has no clear conception of Justification may be saved" and "a Mystic who denies Justification by Faith (Mr Law, for instance) may be saved". Is it not time for us to return to the plain word, "He that feareth God and worketh righteousness is accepted with him?"[38]

There is more to be said in Bunyan's defence than a person of our time may imagine. His emphasis throughout is on "spirit". These good works, dutiful observances and well-ordered lives stoke the fires of hell if they are "done in a Legal Spirit", that is, if the nature and mercy of God are limited to the keeping of commandments and faith is a business transaction rather than a personal relationship (a covenant of works), and the spirit, the inward disposition, is of no concern provided the rules are kept and the bargain honoured. For Bunyan this was not a conclusion from theory but from life with professing Christians. Though but a decade from profanity and less than half that in the Church, he was painfully aware that many Church members were but legalists with no understanding of grace. He had experienced this in the bitter controversies over baptism which would dog him for the rest of his life. Paedo-Baptists and Believers Baptists were equally at fault:

> . . . we have also some that say, unless your infants be baptized they cannot be saved; and others say, unless you be rightly baptized, you have no ground to be assured that you are believers, or members of Churches; which is so far off from being so good as a Legal Spirit, that it is the Spirit of Blasphemy; as is evident, because they do reckon that the Spirit, Righteousness, and Faith of Jesus, and the confession thereof, is not sufficient to declare men to be members of the Lord Jesus; when on the other side though they be rank hypocrites, yet if they do yield an outward subjection to this or that, they are accounted presently communicable members; which doth clearly discover, that there is not so much honour given to the putting on the righteousness of the Son of God, as there is given to that which a man may do, and

yet go to hell within an hour after; nay, in the very doing of it, doth shut himself for ever from Jesus Christ.[39]

There is more to be said on Bunyan's behalf. We should not discourage people from the desideratum of the Book of Common Prayer that "we may hereafter live a godly, righteous and sober life"; and we cannot all go through the spiritual struggles of a Bunyan or a Wesley; but we ought not to forget that in the sight of the all-holy God and before the "torn wretchedness" of Christ on the cross our good deeds may be as unworthy of acceptance as our sins.[40] They too need forgiveness.[41] Tenderness of heart, so much a characteristic of Bunyan himself, is the root of all. The merciful obtain mercy and forgive as they have been forgiven. It is those arrogant in their virtue, contemptuous of the weak, hating sinners, who are excluded eternally from the presence of the God who is love.

Bunyan is inexorable. There is no hope of salvation if one goes to Christ in a "Legal and Old-Covenant Spirit", with a long ledger of self-improvement and a tally of deeds well done, sacraments received, prayers said. This is hypocrisy and self-deceit, a total failure to realise what one is really like; it is a trifling with God and with grace, a making of Christ "a painted Saviour or a Cipher":

> Thou must therefore, if thou wilt so lay hold of Christ, as not to be rejected by him, I say thou must come to him as the basest in the world, more fitter to be damned, if thou hadst thy right than to have the least smile, hope, or comfort from him: come with the fire of hell in thy conscience; come with thy heart hard, dead, cold, full of wickedness and madness against thine own salvation; come as renouncing all thy tears, prayers, watchings, fastings; come as a blood-red sinner, do not stay from Christ, till thou hast a greater own misery, nor of the reality of God's mercy; do not stay while thy heart is softer, and thy spirit in a better frame, but go against thy minde, and against the minde of the devil, and sin, throw thyself down at the foot of Christ with a halter about thy neck, and say, Lord Jesus hear a sinner, a hard-hearted sinner, a sinner that deserveth to be damned, to be cast to hell; and resolve never to return, or to give over crying unto him till thou do finde, that he hath washed thy conscience from dead works with his blood vertually, and clothed thee with his own righteousness, and made thee compleat in himself, this is the way to come to Christ.[42]

"This is the way" for some, ridden by guilt of real or imagined sins. But should such feelings be induced? Modern psychologists would think this highly dangerous, leading a man or woman to a perilous voyage between the Scylla of suicide and the Charybdis of crime; and Bunyan himself, as we have seen, knows how terrible a state is despair, in which one must not be left for a moment longer than is necessary for a glimpse of hell. That is why he urges his unregenerate reader not to linger in wretchedness but to go to Christ immediately, just as he or she is. We may recognise that Christ may speak mercy through an analyst as well as a pastor, or any forgiven sinner whose burden has rolled away. This is the value of Bunyan's theology for our time, not that we should grovel in our guilt or make Giant Despair's castle into a home, but go where there is deliverance, to where God himself has entered totally into our hopelessness that we might be for ever free.

It will be objected by some that this is a narrowly individualist understanding of salvation. Perhaps they forget that the psychiatrists' consulting rooms are full, but it is true that there has been, at least since the Holocaust and the dropping of the atom bomb, a sense among some thoughtful and sensitive people of cosmic despair. Is not the history of our planet a tragedy? This is deplored by others, influenced in various ways by Marxism. The old Stalinists would say that "we welcome our theologies of despair simply because they confirm us in (a) nightmare refusal of revolt; they are our necessary dope"[43] Recent Liberation theologians would similarly attack emphasis on the tragic elements in Christianity, the sufferings of Jesus, the cry of forsakeness on the cross, as condemning the oppressed to perpetual servitude in modern equivalents of ancient Egypt, whereas the gospel is deliverance of the captive and good news for the poor. And this is not primarily a message of hope to depressed and guilt-ridden individuals. Both their condition and our preoccupation with them may be part of our bourgeois malaise. It is a social gospel.

The rebuke is not to go unheeded; yet a belief in the Easter victory which ignores the darkness of the cross may lack compassion for the poor and oppressed, and revolutionary violence bring most suffering to those least able to bear it, as well as being inspired by a Utopianism which disregards both Christian eschatology (the victory is God's at the end) and the relativities of the human scene. Too often the result is a tyranny worse than that which has been overthrown. We cannot evade "the costliness of historical action" or "the unconsoled nature of historical pain". And in the cross of Christ we see him as in some sense a tragic victim, entering into the pain of human life and history, but it is God-in-Christ who hangs and suffers there, even in Christ's seeming abandonment by God, and we are freed from despair because of his presence in absence and the union with the human race, which is an ontological fact even though our lack of faith blinds us to its reality. And this outpouring of the divine life in self-giving love and in total identification with the human tragedy is the motive for our action. The work is God's. We kneel awestruck before what he has done, altogether apart from us, and yet this is our inspiration. The Holy Spirit flowing from the Crucified, the divine life imparted to us once we are willing by faith to receive it and not trust merely in our own ideologies and policies, so perverted by our selfish ambition, empowers us to protest against "the world", "the system", to resist its values and compromises, to contend for justice and yet for ever to be conscious of individual pain and the incalculable value of every human being.[44]

In the *The Doctrine of the Law and Grace Unfolded* Bunyan deals at length with the most dreadful case of conscience in which the Christian, though aware of salvation by grace through faith, fears that he may have committed the unpardonable sin against the Holy Spirit. He had known this agony himself, a distress of the bruised and over-tender conscience. The letter to Hebrews with its denial of second repentance tortured Bunyan and many sensitive souls. Bunyan concludes that the sin against the Spirit is the total and deliberate rejection of Christ, the trampling underfoot of the Son of God, the profaning of the blood of the covenant. He fears that Ranters and Quakers may be in danger of it because they deny the objectivity of atonement wrought by Christ and will not "venture the salvation of (their) souls on the blood shed on Mount *Calvary*".

The sin against the Spirit calls Christ's works those of the Devil and denies the Spirit of God in him; it is also a sin against the Spirit which has enlightened us. It resists all motions of the Spirit of goodness within our hearts and:

> all its gentle entreatings of the soul . . . It repudiates the teachings of the apostles and prophets. But, above all, it is wilful. If there is the least vestige in our hearts of desire for Christ, of opposition to sin, of longing for goodness, then we cannot have committed the unpardonable sin. If there be any souls that be but now willing to venture their salvation upon the merits of a naked Jesus, I do verily for the present believe, they have not sinned that sin; because there is still a promise holds forth itself to such a soul, where Christ saith, *He that comes to me, I will in no wise* (for nothing that he hath done) *cast him out.* John 6.37. That promise is worthy to be written in letters of gold.[45]

4

The Uses of Imprisonment

The Commonwealth, whatever its failure in the filling of the void left by regicide, was the most tolerant rule England had known, or was to know for another thirty years. Cromwell, of whom John Buchan rightly said that he was "in essence a mystic" whose religion was based not on fear but on love, had that quality of "tenderness" which is so marked a characteristic of the religion of many Puritans, not least Bunyan himself. In 1652 John Owen had drawn up a scheme for religious settlement and Cromwell remarked that "he had rather that Mahometanism were permitted amongst us than that one of God's children should be persecuted".[1]

There were many, however, who feared toleration for a variety of reasons, not least because it might lead to the surrender of their privileges, an end of the hegemony which sustained the rule of their class. *Ecclesia Anglicana*, beautiful as it was and as George Herbert in his poetry and eloquent writers of theology contended, a *via media* between Rome and extremer systems, was the church of the aristocracy, and from Elizabeth I to the civil wars, of the government. Those who longed for its restoration could brook no rivals. But there were fears, justified by the excesses of the sects at the end of the wars and fed both by their contentions and the growth of the Quakers, that toleration might lead to chaos resulting in a tyranny worse than that of a Stuart king. This is often the consequence of freedom in human history, evidenced in our own time in many parts of the world. Freedom fighters lack realism and demand too much, while they are nearly always bitterly divided among themselves.

Before Cromwell's death in September 1658 there were signs of reaction. A year earlier Bunyan had been indicted for preaching at Eaton Socon, though the case was not proceeded with. In May 1659 he preached in a barn at Toft in Cambridgeshire and his right was challenged by the Professor of Arabic and Cambridge University Librarian, Thomas Smith. Bunyan replied that he had been called by the Church at Bedford. There was some published controversy. William Dell, Master of Gonville and Caius College, Cambridge, and Rector of Yelden, Bedfordshire, had Bunyan to preach at his parish church on Christmas Day 1659, but there was some opposition and in any case Dell was a Puritan, soon to resign his mastership and to be ejected from Yelden in 1662. Meanwhile there had been further controversy with the Quakers over witchcraft. Bunyan himself had been accused by a woman Quaker because he had said that "the man Christ Jesus" was above the clouds; but he accepted with naïve credulity a story that a Quaker witch, Widow Morlin, had turned Margaret Pryor, an occasional attender at meetings, into a mare and ridden on her four miles to a banquet. The pamphlet in which he retailed this and attacked the Quakers, doubtless with his pen dipped in vitriol, has not survived.[2]

Charles II was restored in May 1660. Even before that, the Bedford Congregation, fearful of the consequences, held days of prayer. Charles himself, easy-going by nature, had, largely under the influence of his mother, become convinced while in exile that established Catholicism was the only religion that could sustain the throne and hoped to achieve this by an alliance of anti-Anglicans, using Dissenters as "stalking-horses for Catholic power". [3] As soon as he could, he threw over Clarendon and the Anglicans, who had been so prominent in bringing him back, and moved towards the toleration of the heirs of the Puritans that he might win it for Catholics too; but strong forces against him, combined with his own indolence, made his policy in the late 1660s and early 1670s but intermittently effective. Meanwhile the returning Cavaliers lusted for vengeance against their old enemies and, displaying the ugliest face of Anglicanism, sought with arrogant disdain to destroy any alternative forms of Christianity to their own.

Bunyan continued to preach, though aware of the dangers. On November 12th 1660 he went to Lower Samsell in Bedfordshire. He himself has told of what ensued, in *A Relation of the Imprisonment of Mr John Bunyan*, which was not published until 1765, more than a hundred years later. The local justice, Francis Wingate, had already issued a warrant for his arrest under a statute of Elizabeth I against nonconformity ((35 Eliz. c. 1). Bunyan was told of this by his friends; and "had I minded to have played the coward, I could have escaped, and kept out of his hands". But he would not, for this would not only have betrayed his confidence in the gospel and the word of God, it "might be a discouragement to the whole body that might follow after".

Bedford gaol

Here we come close to the heart of all martyrs: they will not run away. They may well appear irresponsible and to hate those dearest to them (Luke 14:26). Bunyan had married his second wife Elizabeth in 1659 and she had taken on his four children, including the blind daughter; and was herself to miscarry under the strain of the next months. But he was adamant. He would neither evade arrest nor make the concessions which would have secured his liberty. He was urged to do so time and time again. After some altercation in which "an old enemy to the truth, Dr Lindale" joined, Wingate committed him to Bedford gaol; but as he was going there William Foster, commissary and later chancellor of the diocese of Lincoln and a brother-in-law of Wingate's, greeted him with warm affection and besought him to comply with the law by promising "to call the people no more together". They argued, Foster charging Bunyan with ignorance of Scripture since he knew no Greek and was like the papists, tied to a crude literalism, while his people were poor, simple and ignorant whom his preaching distracted from their work. Bunyan was unmoved and when friends failed to procure his release, being refused by a hesitant and timorous Elstow justice, he accepted prison as the divine will, while he awaited the quarter sessions.

There were four justices of whom the soon-to-be-knighted John Kelynge was the chief. He had been imprisoned in Windsor Castle from 1642 to 1660 and his royalist ardour was now seeking revenge. Later zeal, overcoming all pretensions to justice, combined with pert and bawdy humour, seems to have been his undoing. Here there was much dispute about the Book of Common Prayer, which Bunyan refused to hear as not commanded in Scripture. He adduced the arguments, doubtless much rehearsed in his preaching and later written up in the first of the prose works of his imprisonment. *I Will Pray with the Spirit*. Kelynge rejoined by saying that "we might pray with the spirit, and with understanding and with the Common Prayer-book also", which, I suppose, most modern Christians would accept. But Bunyan could not agree that set prayers might also be the work of the Holy Spirit. It is not easy for us to agree with him, but for him the enemy was formal religion, which mumbled a few prescribed and half-understood prayers and thereupon withdrew to the alehouse or worse. Kelynge's howler that "we know the Common Prayer-book hath been ever since the Apostles time" could be interpreted as meaning that there had always been some set forms in the Church. But Kelynge did not think that tinkers should be preachers. Bunyan's vocation was among the pots and pans. Only those learned in the schools and duly authorised should be allowed to preach. And the sentencing which followed would surely make Bunyan tremble if only for a moment:

> You must be had back again to prison, and there lie for three months following; at three months end, if you do not submit to go to church to hear divine service, and leave your preaching, you must be banished the realm: And if, after such a day as shall be appointed you to be gone, you shall be found in this realm, etc, or be found to come over again without special licence from the King etc. you must stretch by the neck for it, I tell you plainly.

There were still attempts to dissuade Bunyan from refusing to conform. Paul Cobb, the clerk to the justices, visited him after three months and pleaded with him to submit and continue to have some opportunity to do good in the land without public meetings or preachments, whereas banishment would exclude him, possibly for ever. Bunyan remembered Wyclif, who had said that "he which leaveth off preaching and hearing of the word of God for fear of excommunication of men, he is already excommunicated of God, and shall in the day of judgement be counted a traitor to Christ". But he thanked Cobb "for his civil and meek discoursing with me" and ends his account with the doubtless heartfelt apostrophe, "O! that we might meet in Heaven!"

Bunyan did not profit from the coronation amnesty in April 1661, being a convicted person, but he was given a year to sue for pardon, which meant that his sentence of banishment was delayed. His wife presented a petition three times on his behalf at the Midsummer Assizes in August 1661 and received some sympathy from Sir Matthew Hale, who was kinder than the other judges yet powerless to overrule the conviction. The majority of the bench thought of Bunyan as "a pestilent fellow" and a mere disturber of the peace. Elizabeth's assurances that he preached but the word of God were unavailing. She felt that he was denied justice because he was a poor man and a tinker. She departed in tears, not for her husband and herself but "to think what a sad account such creatures will have to give at the coming of the Lord".

Bunyan's imprisonment was not very rigorous at first. He was let out on parole to continue preaching as before, exhorting people to remain steadfast in the New Testament faith, warning them against the Book of Common Prayer. He was even allowed to go to London, though this nearly cost his gaoler his job. He was able to read. He became more than ever steeped in the Bible and in John Foxe's *Acts and Monuments*, the "Book of Martyrs" and for Protestants a continuation of the sacred story of Scripture. This would reinforce his Protestant resolution, not unmixed with fears of popery, and his histrionics. There is, however, more to it than that. Foxe, though basically a Calvinist, was influenced by Luther's and Melancthon's theology of history. Foxe himself was an engaging eccentric of Franciscan generosity, some powers of healing mental illness and of extra-sensory perception. A fine preacher and man of prayer, he showed a rare humanitarianism and compassion in interceding for prisoners condemned to the stake, not least for the Jesuit Edmund Campion. He was no preserve of the Puritans. He was read by Francis Drake to his sailors, Nicholas Ferrar to his community at Little Gidding and his book was the first to be extracted for John Wesley's Christian Library.

Writings in prison

Bunyan was able to converse with fellow-prisoners who were mostly there for their faith. They shared in Bible study and exposition. He had frequent visitors, some seeking spiritual guidance. Above all he was allowed to write.

Yet conditions were not those of a twentieth-century luxury hotel. Prisons were privatised, fees had to be paid and the wealthier prisoners could buy privileges which the poorer, like Bunyan, could not afford. There was poor sanitation, overcrowding, inadequate heating, gaol fever, and in 1665 the plague. Only those, like Bunyan, of strong constitution had much chance of survival for any length of time.

There was, worst of all, perpetual uncertainty. Bunyan had been threatened with banishment if not the scaffold and these possible fates, though they receded, hung over him. After the tolerable existence of the first months he seems to have been confined for some years, except for a few months' release in 1666, which, since he resumed his preaching, resulted in his re-arrest. Government policy fluctuated as well as the will to carry it out. For much of the time he was undisturbed, but never secure. As with the early Christians, active persecution was intermittent, but one never knew when the punitive arm of the state might descend. Bunyan never wavered nor gave so much as a nod towards those who would have pardoned him had he compromised ever so slightly. The words of Scripture were now all of assurance, all to the strengthening of his resolve. In his account appended to *Grace Abounding* he does not omit to tell of his moods of despair, especially when he was "but a young Prisoner" torn from his family who were left in poverty, and particularly his "poor, blind child". Even then Scripture helped, not least the Old Testament, the passage about the milch kine having to carry the Ark of God into another country and to leave their calves behind them (1 Samuel 6:10,11,12; and Jeremiah 49:11, "Leave thy fatherless children, I will preserve them alive, and let thy widows trust in me"). He must venture his all on God. The alternative might be the fires of hell.

At first the prospect of the gallows revived all his old doubts about himself. Would he not be a coward at the last, in front of the crowds? Was he fit to die? After many weeks he drew comfort from the recollection that he was, after all, under sentence "for the Word and Way of God". And whether saved by God or not he must stand to God's Word. Doubtless inspired by what he was reading in Foxe:

> Wherefore, thought I, the point being thus, I am for going on and
> venturing my eternal state with Christ, whether I have comfort here or
> no; if God doth not come in, thought I, I will leap off the Ladder even
> blindfold into Eternitie, sink or swim, come heaven, come hell; Lord
> Jesus, if thou wilt catch me, do; if not, I will venture for thy Name.[4]

Bunyan's first works in prison were probably *Profitable Meditations*, a collection of verses; and the pastoral letters which form the *Relation* of his imprisonment, not, as we have seen, published until long after his death. *I Will Pray with the Spirit* was doubtless written white-hot from his altercations with Judge Kelynge, though it would contain the substance of much of his preaching at this time. No copy of the first edition is known, but it may have been published in 1662.

The treatise is an exposition of 1 Corinthians 14:15, "I will pray with the Spirit and I will pray with the understanding also".

> Prayer is a sincere, sensible, affectionate pouring out of the heart or
> soul to God through Christ in the strength and assistance of the Holy
> Spirit, for such things as God hath promised, or, according to the Word,
> for the good of the Church, with submission, in Faith, to the Will of
> God.

Such a definition emphasises the petitionary or "prophetic" nature of prayer rather than the "mystical," to adopt Friedrich Heiler's influential and definitive, though perhaps rather too sharp, dichotomy. There is a tradition which would regard petition as concerned with the "lower levels" of prayer and is somewhat embarrassed by Scripture in consequence, where prayer is largely "prophetic" and the teaching of Jesus is almost entirely an injunction to "Ask! Seek! Knock!" and you will be certain of an answer. Bunyan does say, however, that the essence of prayer is "a detestation of sin" and "a longing desire after Communion with God, in a holy and undefiled state and inheritance", which would find more sympathy from many teachers of our time who would see Communion as primary. Within this our petitions have their place, but as an aspect of the relationship of prayer rather than its *raison d'être*.[5]

Prayer, for Bunyan, seems to be confined, as on Calvinist understanding it must be, to the Church. Is it possible to pray for those who, by unalterable decree, are outside the covenant of Grace, who cannot receive the benefits of Christ or the influences of the gospel because their hearts are eternally hardened? They constitute 'the world' in the pejorative Johannine sense. They are those for whom Jesus does not pray in John 17, "I pray not for the world", which, together with the prayers of Paul, is Bunyan's model.

This "sincere, sensible, affectionate pouring out of the heart or soul to God" cannot be other than in the Spirit. It is incompatible with prayers out of a book, in borrowed words. The contrast with Lancelot Andrewes is fascinating, for he could not presume to address God in his own words, yet his phrases from Scripture and the Fathers on scraps of paper, "slubbered with his pious hands and watered with his penitential tears", are hardly lacking in love for God or pure devotion. Bunyan sneers at those who have:

> both the *Manner and Matter* of their Prayers at their finger ends; setting such a Prayer for such a day, and that twenty years before it comes. One for *Christmass*, another for *Easter*, and six dayes after that. They have also bounded how many syllables must be said in every one of them at their public Exercises. For each Saints day also, they have them ready for the generations yet unborn to say. They can tell you also when you shall kneel, when you should stand, when you should abide in your seats, when you should go up into the Chancel, and what you should do when you come there. All which the Apostles came short of, as not being able to compose so profound a matter.[6]

That is caricature, yet not without warning to those who set their all on prescribed forms or impose them on others, denying all freedom. Not all Puritans had such aversion to the Book of Common Prayer, which in its 1552 and 1559 versions is at heart a very Protestant set of services, with its insistence on the one unrepeatable sacrifice of Christ, and its lavish use of Scripture. The likes of Laud, Andrewes and Cosin had made its rituals more seemly and ceremonious and it had retained some vestiges of medieval worship. It had become for the more extreme Puritans like the brazen serpent in the Jerusalem temple, which King Josiah hewed in pieces; and it was above all about to be an instrument of persecution. But Bunyan's strictures reveal a weakness of Puritan ecclesiology and attitudes to worship. They lacked a sense of historical development and assumed not only that the New Testament was a handbook of worship, but that liturgy could have remained as it was in the apostles' time.

Prayer without the Spirit is, for Bunyan, blasphemy. By nature we are infirm, yet we cannot truly know our misery for we are cold and dead, unless the Spirit give us life. Paul says we do not know how we ought to pray or what to pray for until the Spirit helps us. So prayers cannot be prescribed in advance. Yet the Spirit's first prayers in us are unutterable groanings, for once we are enlightened as to our true state we would fly from God. But the Spirit intercedes for us and gives us confidence even in our wretchedness. He shows us the right way of coming to God, through Christ, and enables us boldly to call God "Father" as the born-again children of God. To babble the Lord's Prayer is no salvation. "No, here is the life of Prayer, when in, or with the Spirit, a man being made sensible of sin, and how to come to the Lord for mercy; he comes, I say, in the strength of the Spirit, and cryeth *Father*." The Lord's Prayer is no "stinted form", or there would not be two versions, one in Matthew, the other in Luke. It is a rule of prayer that we should pray in faith, to God in the heavens, and for "such things as are according to his Will".[7]

But prayer must be with the understanding also. The Corinthians made their spiritual gifts an occasion for boasting and their prayers were more a display of their extraordinary powers than an edifying of the Church. Understanding means prayer in our mother-tongue. Bunyan does not expound this; it could exclude both the Latin mass and enthusiastic *glossolalia* alike. Understanding means also to pray *experimentally* – to know our wants, to know God's willingness to save sinners; and to marshall our arguments, for prayer is not without disputation; it is even a wrestling with God and "an engine against the Almighty", to quote George Herbert as Bunyan does not; though the Almighty himself has devised it for us, since he has destined us, not for mystical absorption in the infinite, but for a dynamic relationship of living beings with a living God.

This is a bald summary and paraphrase of Bunyan's usual plethora of expository points. He answers objections and with great pastoral encouragement in the main, though when he deals with the contention "if we do not use set forms of prayer, how shall we teach our Children to pray?" his child psychology is hardly that of our time and may appal us. We should begin by telling our children what accursed creatures they are, and how they are under the wrath of God by reason of original and actual sin. To give them forms of prayer before they know this is to make them hypocrites.

> Learn therefore your Children to know their wretched state and condition; tell them of hell fire, and their sins, of damnation, and salvation: the way to escape the one, and to enjoy the other (if you know it yourselves) and this will make tears run down your sweet babes eyes, and hearty groans flow from their hearts; and then also you may tell them to whom they should pray, and through whom they should pray . . .

Bunyan addresses a word of reproof to those who never pray at all. This is threatening indeed. "What wilt thou do when thou shalt be damned in Hell, because thou couldst not find in thine heart to ask for Heaven?" But this leads him back to condemnation of the Book of Common Prayer, which is not true prayer "when it hath nothing but the Tradition of men and the strength of Persecution to uphold, or plead for it".

These dire negatives are not, however, his main thrust. Nothing should discourage us from prayer, not our senselessness nor fear, nor the temptations which steal in to pervert and pollute our holy desires. In all we must remember that God hears us from the mercy-seat, sprinkled with the Blood of Jesus to stop the course of divine justice. He concludes with twelve "Words of Advice" to all God's people, telling them *inter alia* to expect temptations which are to be looked for the first day that they enter into Christ, "his Congregation", to be jealous of the deceits of the heart in seeking evidences that we are destined for heaven, to beware flatteries, and to take heed of little sins.[8]

Against the Latitudinarians

The controversy over set forms died down after the early months of Bunyan's imprisonment. The Nonconformists were to have no legal place in English religion or indeed English society as the various measures known as the Clarendon Code were enacted. And Bunyan, confined more strictly, was in no position to contend any more for his right to preach and pray in freedom. His opportunities to remain in contact with the Bedford congregation seem to have been curtailed. This we may imagine as a period of introspection culminating in the publication of *Grace Abounding* in 1666. Bunyan was uncertain as to his fate, anxious about his family, reduced to making "long tagg'd laces" to raise a little money for their needs. At times he was in the slough of despond. On one occasion it was his turn to speak at the prisoners' preachment, but he says that he was "so empty, spiritless and barren that I thought I should not have been able to speak among them so much as five words of truth with life and evidence". But he lighted on Revelation 21 and not only produced a sermon out of it, but "after we had well dined, I gathered up this basketful . . . of the fragments that were left". These were considerable and the result was *The Holy City* (1665).

There are various possible reactions to what Christopher Hill has called "the experience of defeat". One is to conspire politically and plot revolution. This happened frequently in Charles II's reign and notably in the early years in Venner's Fifth Monarchy rising of January 1661. It was fierce and frightening. Bunyan had no truck with this or any other plot, though John Owen seems to have been involved in some conspiracies which proposed violence, since guns were found in his London home. Bunyan was never an advocate of violence through all the many planned uprisings.

An alternative to armed rebellion is eschatology. The Revelation of John, from which Bunyan takes the vision of the Holy City, was an attempt to keep up the spirits of persecuted Christians, who had no force of arms, in assurance of the reign and vengeance and final triumph of God. Bunyan became a millenarian in his theology of history while he also re-fought the battle within. In spite of occasional depressions he was almost exuberant about his lot. Prison was a school of immortality, a means of the Spirit's triumph.

> I never had in all my life so great an inlet into the Word of God as now; then Scriptures that I saw nothing in my life before, are made in this place and start to shine upon me; Jesus Christ also was never more real or apparent than now; here I have seen him and felt him indeed.[9]

In *The Holy City* Bunyan writes as though the thousand-year reign of the saints preparatory to the return of Christ was near, though he does not specify a date. The persecution of the Nonconformists is part of the inaugural time of tribulation. "The church in the fire of persecution is like Esther in the perfuming chamber, but making fit for the presence of the King."[10] Monarchs and governments will often be the strongest opponents of the rule of Christ, but Bunyan does not discount the possibility of their final submission after the cosmic struggle, in which the Church's warfare seems to be spiritual.

Two other works of his imprisonment, *One Thing is Needful*, and *The Resurrection of the Dead*, are also eschatological. But the inner conflict seems to have most preoccupied him until near the end of his twelve-year time, when he found a new adversary in the Anglican Edward Fowler, Rector of Northill just outside Bedford. Fowler had been a Puritan and was ejected in 1662, but after some hesitation conformed. He was preferred to a London living in 1672 and later became Bishop of Gloucester, where he showed a less temporising spirit by refusing to read out James II's Declaration of Indulgence. As one of those opprobriously called "Latitude men", he represented the new movement in the English Church, which we have already noted. Fowler and his like were much despised as turncoats, but we must not deny their convictions, and the future was with them. They originated in the universities, especially Cambridge, though Fowler was an Oxford man. They were part of the reaction against Calvinism which began in the 1640s and 1650s and makes a fascinating study in itself, not least as a development from Puritanism. Isabel Rivers does not think that they should be distinguished from the Cambridge Platonists and Fowler quotes John Smith; but although they had a like emphasis on reason – "I oppose not rational to spiritual; for spiritual is most rational," said Whichcote – I would feel that they lacked the mystical element so dominant in the Platonists, the sense of mystery at the heart of the Christian faith, even though theirs was an intellectual mysticism and not in the tradition of Dionysius the Areopagite.[11]

In 1670 Fowler published *The Principles and Practices of Certain Moderate Divines of the Church of England*, but the work Bunyan read in prison and answered was its sequel, *The Design of Christianity; or, A Plain Demonstration and Improvement of this Proposition, viz. That the Enduing men with Inward Real Righteousness or True Holiness was the Ultimate End of our Saviour's Coming into the World, and is the Great Intendment of His Blessed Gospel.*

Fowler's concern is with holiness. Here we may find a parallel with the Platonists for whom the imitation of Christ was central and who succeeded better than most in translating this into their lives, but there are again differences. Fowler is much more akin to classical moralists than to the Reformation divines. Holiness is human nature at its best, the restoration of innate qualities. It does not seem to demand radical change, certainly not in society. Those in whom holiness resides will "demean themselves suitably to that state in which God has placed them and not . . . act disbecomingly in any Condition, Circumstance or Relation". It is behaviour in accordance with reason and not sensual imagination or brutish passions. Christ brings us to holiness as we follow his example. Fowler's is the Christology of the perfect gentleman, a portrait painted from a very selective reading of the gospels, interpreted by what had then become the Anglican virtues; it perhaps deserves George Tyrrell's well-known criticism of Harnack and the Liberal Protestants that its vision of Christ is that of its own face seen at the bottom of a deep well.

Fowler defines justifying faith in a way sufficient to call up Luther from his grave: "*It is such a belief in the truth of the Gospel, as includes a sincere resolution of Obedience unto all its Precepts;* or, (which is the same thing) includes *true Holiness* in the nature of it.*"* He is fearful of Antinomianism to which he thinks the doctrine of justification by faith alone tends. He is after an inward and real righteousness and is afraid that the doctrine that, accepted by God through Christ, we are treated as though we were already righteous, will deceive us into imagining that works do not matter. What is essential is a sincere desire for holiness and holiness is happiness, to use a phrase beloved of John Wesley, who has more in common with the Latitude men than is sometimes thought, though he disowned them. Fowler possibly does not understand the psychology of imputed righteousness, that as we are treated as righteous we become righteous, as we put on Christ over our unlovely nakedness we are changed into his beauty.[12]

Bunyan replied to Fowler in the last work of his first imprisonment with a title long even by seventeenth-century standards: *A Defence of the Doctrine of Justification by Faith in Jesus Christ; shewing, True Gospel-Holiness flows from Thence; or, Mr Fowler's Pretended Design of Christianity, Proved to be nothing more than to trample under Foot the Blood of the Son of God; and the Idolizing of Man's own Righteousness.*

He is very contemptuous and regards Fowler as little more than a heathen with a naïve faith in the innate goodness of human nature belied both by Scripture and experience. Christ is Saviour not primarily exemplar, or, as Fowler makes him, schoolmaster. He is inimitable in his role as mediator and the one sacrifice for sin, though exemplary to the justified by virtue of his meekness and self-denial. Bunyan does not spare insults. He who had resisted conformity to the point of exile or death cannot abide the seeming turncoat. Fowler would be a Mahometan in Turkey. He is "a glorious Latitudinarian, that can, as to religion, turn and twist like an eel on the angle; or rather like the weathercock that stands on the steeple . . . Your book, Sir, is begun in ignorance, managed with error, and ended in blasphemy."[13]

Fowler abandoned all pretensions to temperance and irenical moderation in his, or his curate's, reply. It was entitled *Dirt Wip't Off; A manifest Discovery of the gross Ignorance, erroneousness and most UnChristian and Wicked Spirit of one John Bunyan.* It is interesting, however, that Richard Baxter in his reply to Fowler, *How Far Holiness is the Design of Christianity*, felt that his work was needed against the "disease" of Antimonianism, "an erroneous crying up the Gospel and crying down the Law". He called Bunyan "an unlearned Antinomian-Anabaptist", yet in his comprehensiveness regarded him as a true Christian: "I never heard that Bunnian was not an honest, godly man. If then he attained the design of Christianity, was he not a Christian?"[14]

Baxter's "Catholic Spirit" must not deceive us into thinking that Bunyan and Fowler are travelling the same road home to God. Isabel Rivers has superbly summarised the issues:

> For Bunyan religious language and religious narrative involve drawing
> distinctions, defining opposites, and identifying enemies. The tendency
> in the writing of the latitude-men on the other hand is to conflate
> terms: grace and virtue, faith and works, religion and happiness – these
> are but one and the same thing, to use a favourite latitudinarian phrase.
> For Bunyan religion is about salvation to glory in the next world. The
> consequence of justification by faith is a life of holiness in this world,
> but holiness has nothing to do with rewards, in this world or the next.
> It may bring content, but is more likely to bring suffering; the religious
> man will more often go in rags than in silver slippers, be bound in
> irons than walk in the streets with applause. For the latitude-men
> religion is about two things, reason and morality. To understand the
> relation of man to God and to live the morally good life in the light
> of that understanding will bring about happiness in this world as well
> as the next. Those who choose to suffer mistake the nature of religion.
> The assumptions of these two different versions of Christianity were
> incomprehensible to each other.[15]

Bunyan's long imprisonment then ended in controversy as it began, its vehemence undiminished. But the years and the apprehensions, the weary waiting in uncertain deprivation, the moods of exultation and depression, had given to the world the author of *The Pilgrim's Progress*.

5
Bunyan and his Church

On 15th March 1672 there was a Royal Declaration of Indulgence and Bunyan was released from prison the same month. Fowler in his rage against Bunyan's attack on his *Design* had thought the Declaration should not apply to him. His freedom was actually obtained through his name being added to a petition on behalf of nearly five hundred Quakers, which is ironic in view of his fierce opposition to them. On the preceding 21st January he had been appointed Pastor of the Bedford Congregation. From late 1668 he had been allowed to make forays from prison and had become involved in Nonconformists' attempts to organise themselves in preparation for some measure of liberty. There was no long, untroubled respite. The Declaration was cancelled in 1673, attendant licences were revoked in 1675, Bunyan was again in prison from December 1676 to June 1677 (this time his release was due in part to the good offices of John Owen); and until the death of Charles II in 1685 Nonconformists existed uneasily, not least because of official paranoia of Catholic conspiracies. In *Israel's Hope Encouraged*, published posthumously in 1692, he wrote of "days of trouble, especially since the discovery of the Popish Plot, for then we began to fear cutting of Throats, of being burned in our beds, and of seeing our children dashed in pieces before our Faces".

The Bedford Congregation had been founded in 1650 by "holy Mr Gifford", a converted Royalist officer. We have already noted his influence on the young Bunyan, and although he lived only until 1655 he determined the ethos of the congregation. Separated from "prelatical superstition", it was almost Miltonic in its tolerance and belief that truth could never be worsted in a free and open encounter. From his deathbed Gifford wrote beseeching his congregation to "avoid all disputes which gender to strifes, as questions about externals and all doubtful disputations". Psalm-singing, condemned by the Quakers among others as an unscriptural distraction from true waiting on God, was a thing indifferent. Disagreements over baptism were to be tolerated. On these questions Bunyan followed in Gifford's steps, as we shall see.

Gifford also held strongly that all believers were equal before God, who was no respecter of persons. "When you are met as a church, there's neither rich nor poor, bond nor free, in Christ Jesus".[1]

The congregation was not composed entirely of social inferiors, as its detractors supposed. Christopher Hill has used various sources, original and otherwise, to show that while "in 1669 Bunyan's meeting was described as Anabaptist, having about thirty members of the 'meanest sort' – shopkeepers and craftsmen, hatters, cobblers, heelmakers", there were several who were prominent in Bedford civic politics, two or three mayors and two Triers for the Cromwellian state church.[2]

It may be said that from the day of his first encounter with the poor women talking of the things of God and acquaintance with John Gifford, the Church at Bedford was the great support and joy of Bunyan's life. It was "the good Providence of God" that brought him there. Throughout his writings there is a very clear doctrine of the Church, the communion of saints, who are the apple of God's eye. Post-Tridentine Catholics misunderstand Bunyan if they feel that he lacks a concept of the Church, because it is for him no ordered hierarchy. It is rather the fellowship of believers. And Christ and his Church are one. "For God, and Christ, and his People are so linked together, that if the Good of one be prayed for, to wit, the Church, the glory of God, and the advancement of Christ must needs be included."[3] "Church fellowship rightly managed is the glory of the world."[4]

In his tract from prison, *Christian Behaviour* (1663), he describes the Church as a garden, an ordered garden, in which the flowers "stand and grow where the gardener hath planted them": "Christians are like the several flowers in a garden, that have upon each of them the dew of heaven, which being shaken with the wind, they let fall their dew at each other's roots, whereby they are jointly nourished and become nourishers of one another." The simile is also found in *The Pilgrim's Progress*, Part II, where Christiana and her companions are taken into the Interpreter's garden and shown the flowers. He tells them: "Behold the Flowers are divers in *Stature*, in *Quality*, and *Colour* and *Smell* and *Virtue*, and some are better than some: Also where the gardener hath set them, there they stand, and quarrel not with one another."[5]

The Palace Beautiful in *The Pilgrim's Progress* is Bunyan's picture of the Church, where the pilgrim is received with courtesy and given rest in the chamber called Peace, though not without enquiry as to his credentials.

He talks over his Christian life with the virtuous girls who live there – Discretion, Piety, Charity and Prudence – and he has supper at a table "furnished with fat things and with Wine that was well refined; and all their talk was about the Lord of the Hill; as namely about what he had done and wherefore he did what he did".[6]

Beautiful is the repository of the holy and living tradition, the records of the past, and the promise and hope of the future. It gives a vision of the Delectable Mountains, from which, when the pilgrims arrive, they may glimpse the Celestial City. It is a museum of the heroes of old, but also the armoury where the pilgrim is equipped for the warfare ahead. And he leaves with a viaticum of bread and wine and raisins.

The young are catechised at Palace Beautiful. And there is further sacramental allusion in the pills which are given to cure certain distempers – *ex Carne et Sanguine Christi* – which echoes the tradition going back to Ignatius of Antioch, who within a generation of the New Testament refers to the Eucharist as "the medicine of immortality".[7]

There is rapture at the Lord's table. The ordinances of the Church are the pledges of God's presence, "his love-letters and love-tokens too". The true Christian loves to be at the breaking of bread where Christ, as at Emmaus, makes himself known. Here is feasting "made for mirth".

Did Bunyan share the rapture of Agnes Beaumont, a member of the Bedford Church from neighbouring Edworth, with whom he innocently and reluctantly committed his one recorded indiscretion with a woman, when, in 1674, he took her riding pillion behind him to a meeting at Gamlingay? He did this only at her brother's insistence. She herself has told the story:

> And so we came to Gamlingay, and after a while the meeting began and made it a blessed meeting to my soul indeed. Oh, it was a feast of fat things to me. My soul was filled with consolation and I sat under His shadow with great delight and His fruit was pleasant to my taste when I was at the Lord's table . . . I found such a return of prayer I was scarce able to bear up under it . . . Oh, I had such a sight of Jesus Christ that brake my heart to pieces . . . a sense of my sins and of His dying love made me love Him and long to be with Him: and truly it was infinite condescension in Him and I have often thought of His gracious goodness to me that Jesus Christ should so visit my poor soul that day.

The journey did not pass unobserved, nor without consequences. Agnes writes, "A priest . . . lookt of us as, wee rode Along the way as if he would have staird his eyes out". And when she returned home, "Ploshing through the durt over shoes, haueing noe pattings on" her father "was very Angry with me, for rideing behind Mr Bunyan, and said I should never come within his doores Againe, Except I would promise him to leave going after that man". She could not agree to desist, "it was like death to me to bee kept from such a Meeting". But a few days after the angry confrontation her father died and her suitor, jealous of her friendship with Bunyan, charged her with poisoning him. There was a coroner's inquest and a jury. Both Geoffrey Nuttall and Gordon Rupp find it all rather amusing in retrospect, the latter comparing the inquest to Gilbert and Sullivan's *Trial by Jury*; the coroner "could not be too kind and encouraging". But it would be tense at the time. Agnes herself became a notable preacher.[8]

The Communion rapture and the whole incident raise once more the question of sexuality and religion, of eros and agape. We may ignore any carnal desires as not consciously present, but it could be that the excitement of the journey with Bunyan, to whom she almost certainly had one of those pastoral relationships which lead either to rapturous devotion to the things of God or intense sexual expression, heightened the joy and penitence and consolations of the Lord's table. There may be ways from the fellowship of the gathered Church and the influence of gifted pastors, either to the Celestial City or to hell.

Bunyan was well aware that Palace Beautiful might be vandalised by scandals, by *odium theologicum*, by disputes over trifles or by quarrels among members. As we have seen (above p. 61), he warns "all God's people" to look for temptations the first day they enter "into Christ, his congregation". Church membership is no insurance policy against falling into sin. The Devil is especially on the watch for saints.

As Pastor he was responsible for discipline. His successor, Ebenezer Chandler, praised the "Accuracy of his Knowledge in Church-discipline, and readiness to put that in practice in the Church (as occasion offered) which he saw was agreeable to the Word of God, whether Admonition or Excommunication". The *Minutes* of the Congregation describe meetings, perhaps sometimes uncomfortably reminding one of George Eliot's *Silas Marner*, in which members are arraigned for absence from Church, Sabbath-breaking, card-playing, lying, debt, fraud, railing, brawling and wife-beating.

The tragedy of Dissent was its deep divisions, the bitter controversies, arguments "mixed with gall", which bade fair to destroy not edify. So many of these, as in Christendom as a whole, have been about the sacraments. Bunyan preferred to speak of "Ordinances" rather than sacraments, a term more biblical and redolent of divine authority.[9] As we have reason to know, he regarded these as obligations and very precious, conveyances of Christ in his fullness; but they do not of themselves save us.

> Baptism and the Lord's Supper both, were made for us and not we for them . . . I count them not the fundamentals of our Christianity, nor grounds or rule to communion with saints; servants they are and our mystical ministers, to teach and instruct us in the most weighty matters of the kingdom of God.

Whether Bunyan may be called a Baptist or not is still a matter of dispute. He may himself have been re-baptised on becoming a member of John Gifford's congregation, but there is evidence that his baby daughter Elizabeth was baptised at Elstow in 1654, and an infant son, Joseph, at St Cuthbert's, Bedford in 1672, while when he applied for preaching licences in the latter year he called himself "Congregationall". But Baptists were "Congregationall" in polity, and earlier Richard Baxter had thought of Anabaptists as differing from Congregationalists solely "in pt. of Worshipp".[10] It is most satisfactory to conclude that Bunyan was "an open-membership Baptist", or as his biographer, John Brown, put it "a Baptist of a very mild type".[11]

In two works, *A Confession of My Faith and a Reason of My Practice* (1672); and a reply to outraged reactions against it, *Differences in Judgement about Water-Baptism no Bar to Communion*, Bunyan states his position. He opposes the exclusiveness of those Baptists who would have made a new law out of baptism by asserting that any other than believer's baptism was direst heresy. The "one baptism" of Ephesians 4:5 is no liturgy, but the baptism of the Spirit, and this is what is vital. Love not baptism is the badge of Christ and love is more truly revealed when we receive his children for the sake of Christ than when we refuse them for want of water.

Bunyan's tolerance and charity spring from hatred of those controversies which destroy not edify, which make idols of ordinances and split hairs over ceremonies. The error of the extreme and exclusive Baptists is identical with that of ritualistic High Churchmen. They are like those condemned by Jesus Christ who tithe mint and anise and cummin and neglect judgement and the love of God. He deems the Supper the greater sacrament about which Scripture is more explicit. "The Church as a Church is much more concerned in that than in water-baptism both as to her faith and comfort; both as to her union and communion."[12]

The true Church is, of course, a gathered Church. And communion – by which Bunyan means more than receiving of the supper though that is implied – must be with "visible saints", those who are regenerate and separated in their manner of life from the profane. These latter are pitied rather condescendingly; but they are not scorned "as men". Yet no more than iron can be mixed with miry clay can the saints mix with them "in the worship of God and the fellowship of the gospel".[13]

The ideal of the gathered Church is noble, inspiring and in some ways essential to Christianity, as Stephen Neill and Geoffrey Nuttall have shown.[14] In the end the Church on earth must inevitably be the Catholic *corpus mixtum* and in the small, close-knit community there are many and great dangers, of holier-than-thou, of too great a rigorism, of "want of love", of illicit love, of being lured by the world even in aversion from it. But in the Bedford congregation, in spite of the transgressions of discipline, there are glimpses of a community of mutual care and of the love of Christ, of tolerance in non-essentials, in which upholders of infant baptism and its opponents can worship together and all find the liberty which the Spirit gives. There is a ministry in the gathered Church. The Giffords and the Bunyans are not ostensibly lords of faith but helpers of joy, yet they lead from the front, though not so far from the front that the weakest and slowest lose touch with them. In Part II of *The Pilgrim's Progress* there is no more noble figure than Great-heart: the magnanimous man in the sense of Philippians 4:5, the soldier who fights giants on behalf of his pilgrim band; the exemplar of patient endurance who leads his people to the gate of heaven and returns again and again to fetch more; the expositor able to unravel the knottiest theological problem or case of conscience, who proceeds by dialogue not simply monologue. Such was Gifford and such Bunyan. The latter had a much wider ministry than that of Bedford. He was much in demand as a preacher in London, where it is said he could draw 1200 on a weekday morning and 3000 on Sundays. But the base of his work and the foundation of its stability was the Bedford Congregation, now known as Bunyan Meeting.

6

The Pilgrim's Progress Part I

Bunyan's masterpiece has its antecedents in his own experience, his dire spiritual struggles, his theological disputes, his deliverance from imprisonment within his tortured self, his imprisonment in Bedford gaol. And just as James Joyce's novel *Ulysses*, itself a "spiritual encyclopaedia", exhibits extensive parallels with Homer's *Odyssey* so that the plot set in early twentieth-century Dublin transfers the old classical plot to a new and contemporary scene, so underlying the journey of Bunyan's pilgrims is that of the Children of Israel from the bondage of Egypt to the Promised Land. There is a like "allegorical geography".[1]

There were also the antecedents of medieval pilgrimages. These were regarded by the Protestant Reformers as "fooleries" at best, and at worst occasions of gross superstition and scandal, tending to idolatry, the veneration of images and relics and to immoral behaviour by the way. On 9th June 1536 Hugh Latimer, in a sermon before the Convocation of the clergy, denounced them as superstitious and without warrant of Scripture and in 1538 Henry VIII required all those who had extolled pilgrimages to make public retractions. They were effectively undermined by an injunction of Elizabeth I in 1559, while her first Archbishop, Matthew Parker, utterly disallowed "wanderings on pilgrimages". But, as J. G. Davies has pointed out, this led to "the full interiorisation" of the concept of pilgrimage, beginning with Latimer himself who in Lincolnshire in 1552 preached on "the Christian man's pilgrimage", which he was quick to contrast with popish runnings hither and thither to shrines.[2]

As Davies says, this reached its "full flowering" in Bunyan. He spiritualises what his Protestant and evangelical conscience makes him condemn in the body – music and dancing, feasting and pilgrimages. But behind all is the journeying instinct of humanity. "Home is where one starts from" and to which one returns, though it may not be as one has known it, rather "heaven, the heart's true home", for Christians the home "with the Lord".

But human beings are relentless travellers in imagination even if the circumstances of their lives have not enabled the great majority to go far from
their own communities. Men and women must "out" even if only by
story-telling. They must venture, they must explore, they must have some
sort of a goal, even if for some, in R. L. Stevenson's phrase, "to travel
hopefully is better than to arrive". And this is certainly true of the intellectual quest. A theologian friend has told me privately that the summation
of her life's work could be a book called "Journey into the Indeterminate".
It seems to be a fact of human nature that we must live by faith and that
only so do we attain the full stature of our humanity. And this is com-
pounded by our mortality. We are on a journey whether we like it or not
from birth to death. But there is the tragic addition throughout the ages,
and never more than in our own time, of countless millions who have no
other choice than to be travellers. The poor, the homeless, the refugees
have no abiding city and are menaced by giants of all kinds from oppressive
governments, tyrannous or just incompetent in the face of almost impossible tasks, to multi-national corporations. The journey is the truest metaphor of human life.

Dag Hammarskjold wrote that "the longest journey is the journey
inwards"[3] and mystical writers have used the metaphor, notably Bonaventure in his thirteenth-century *Journey of the Soul to God*. Bonaventure's
journey is contemplative. It is not inward in the sense that it shuts out the
world; rather it is the Franciscan opening of the eyes to see and praise God
in all creatures. Yet contemplation is possible only through the door of the
Lamb's blood and "there is no other path but through the burning love of
the Crucified". This transformed Paul so that he could say "With Christ
I am nailed to the cross. I live, now, not I but Christ lives in me".
Bonaventure cannot but regard this testimony as deriving directly from
Paul's being carried up to the third heaven, as he records in 2 Corinthians
12: 1ff. Received Pauline scholarship would be inclined to think that Bonaventure is conflating Galatians and 2 Corinthians and that in the latter passage
in any case Paul is rather disassociating himself from the mystic vision of
fourteen years previously, which may have elated him unduly. The thorn
in the flesh has taught him more of the sufficiency of grace than did the
unspeakable raptures of paradise; and the divine strength is made perfect,
not in visions and revelations of the Lord, but in weakness. Yet one of
Paul's latest expositors, the Jewish scholar, A. F. Segal, is convinced that
the clue to his whole experience and theology is in his mysticism.[4]

It is interesting that there is a marginal reference to 2 Corinthians 12: 9,
"My grace is sufficient for thee; for my strength is made perfect in weak-

ness", in the account of Christian at the Interpreter's house, when he is shown the fire against a wall which burns higher and hotter, though water is being poured on it. Behind the wall stands a man pouring on oil, the oil of grace. Roger Sharrock has said that here an ordinary farmyard bonfire does duty for the mystic flame.[5] There is here, and elsewhere in Bunyan, George Herbert's "Heaven in Ordinary". It would be wrong to say that there is nothing of the mystic in Bunyan with his acute ear and eye, his imagination so strong, his awareness of Christ so intimate. But for him the journey is undertaken not through contemplative union with Christ in his passion as through the deliverance which the passion, the objective work of divine Grace, brings, and the divine possession of the soul through the purchase of Christ's blood.

He has to justify his method in his verse "Apology" for *The Pilgrim's Progress*. There are those who advised against publishing. The allegory would but darken understanding and confuse simple people who want solid, plain truth. "Metaphors make us blind." He seeks to refute these by pointing out the variety of "engines" by which a fisherman may seek to make his catch, or a fowler lay his snares; and "was not God's Laws/His Gospel-laws in older time set forth/By Types, Shadows and Metaphors?" He needs no precedent other than the Lord Christ's speaking in parables. He is very confident that his allegory will interest, entertain and thus instruct in the way to heaven.

It is interesting that he should seek to please the imagination at a time when the word was often pejoratively used to mean fancy, or as in the Authorised Version's translation of *Magnificat*, "vain conceit". And his method singles out the separatists from the new Churchmen as we have seen, for the Latitudinarians eschewed allegory and typology. And they were particularly scathing about the marginal notes needed to explicate the dark allusions and metaphors, which deceived "the simple and credulous, who persuaded themselves that the cause of those men stood upon the ground of God's word, which they had so ready at their finger's end".[6] But about all this, Bunyan now has no qualms.

He is also convinced that the Christian speaks a language different from that of the world, "the language of Canaan", which, says Rivers, "Implies both a particular pattern for the Christian life . . . and a dependence on Scripture for vocabulary, allusion, metaphor, and literary method."[7] This is particularly pertinent in Bunyan's case, one of whose unregenerate characteristics had been foul-mouthed swearing. But it went against the Latitudinarian fashion of turning the metaphors and idioms of Scripture into plain language. (In this the Latitudinarians were rather like the translators of the Good News Bible in our own time.) They suspected allegories and images as they did the intricacies of theology, which they thought might be sophistries to justify anti-social and immoral behaviour. They wanted, above all, good conduct, a "godly, righteous and sober life", the antithesis of licence, poetic or otherwise. They had much success in the schools, but could not quench the needs of the human imagination, which made *The Pilgrim's Progress* Part I by far the most popular work of seventeenth-century prose fiction and ensured that it would survive the condescending criticisms of Augustan superiority.[8]

"The language of Canaan" has, however, been open to caricature – not least by Charles Dickens in Mr Chadband and Mr Stiggins – and become a term of derision. It has smacked of hypocrisy and been redolent of a style to be avoided if the Christian gospel is to be commended sincerely and honestly in the world. The idea that Christians should speak a special language is contrary to popular conceptions both of Christ and the gospels and of the relevance of Christianity to life. In fact Christ may well have had a special vocabulary, appeared to speak in riddles and was much misunderstood, while the obsession with "relevance" may both bereave Christianity in the next generation and betray its eternal inheritance. And overall is the question whether the human spirit can survive without poetic imagination.[9]

The truth is that Christianity needs several styles of speech and the Latitudinarians have a case. In everyday conversation Christians need to watch their words, to avoid exaggeration and extravagance and those expressions which demean life and degrade both nature and humanity. They must beware the fault of Bunyan's Talkative described in the damning *double entendre* "all he hath lieth in his *tongue*, and his Religion is to make a noise *therewith*". They must learn that most difficult of all demands, to "speak the truth in love". In advocacy and apologetics the language must be suited to the hearers and their thought world. But there is also need for language which recognises the realities beyond time and sense, for which prosaic intelligibility is inadequate, through which alone we may come to terms with the unspeakable hell of existence and the heaven of divine grace and glory. And a certain enjoyment, even merriment, is not precluded provided that life is not seen as a game, either one that we play or one that is being played on us.

Bunyan tells the story of his pilgrims as though seen in a dream. A friend once suggested to Alec Robertson that Newman's poem is called "The *Dream* of Gerontius" because of the lines:

> Thou art wrapped and swathed about in dreams
>   Dreams that are true yet enigmatical,
> For the belongings of thy present state,
>   Save through such symbols come not home to thee.

"In other words the experiences of Gerontius are real but they are like a dream because he does not perceive them through his bodily senses." In *The Pilgrim's Progress* it is not the characters who dream, except occasionally, but the author himself, who sees them with the eye of his imagination and enigmatically. And we must think of it as a "day-dream", "a piece of wish-fulfilment", as every lover knows.[10]

The start

The picture of the man beneath the walls of the City of Destruction with a burden on his back and a book in his hand, crying "What shall I do?" is unforgettable. Bunyan, the tinker, knew what it was to carry a heavy pack as he went from house to house with the tools of his trade. And he had borne the spiritual burden of guilt and been almost crushed by it.

Yet there would be no burden without the book, which is why in the second edition early on his journey, Mr Wordly-Wiseman seeks to dissuade Christian from meddling with biblical mysteries and urges him to tread the plain path to Morality. He speaks for the Latitude men. And there may be those for whom their counsels bring peace of mind. It was one of the errors of Puritanism that everyone must undergo conversion through conviction of sin and the agonised cry of the Philippian gaoler. The doctrine of election made this condition more acute for only a few could be saved in any case. Yet some there are who cannot find deliverance without dire spiritual struggles, like Luther's, to find a gracious God, and to them, as for Bunyan, the book speaks judgement before salvation. It makes their condition worse before it is better.

Today the Bible is mainly read less personally, more as a series of period pieces, which for Christian believers lead to the decisive period of human history which changed the balance of spiritual forces in the universe; but in spite of the revival of evangelicalism and of the vogue for the Ignatian Exercises, fewer feel that it speaks as though it were written for them. And our western, technological age has lost the sense of a divine Judge who punishes iniquity, on reconciliation with whom our true well-being depends not only in this life but after death. If we have a conscience it may be directed more towards our neighbours than God, the poor, the hungry, the exploited, victims of human wickedness and natural disaster. But it is not impossible to think of personal selfishness, disregard of the deprived in the interests of our own prosperity and our involvement in an unjust society as sins against the love which should rule the sun and all the stars. And if belief in God goes, belief in humanity may not long survive. Human life may be cheapened without the belief in the incalculable value which faith in the Christian God gives to it.

But beyond all this, which is a mild attempt to argue for belief in God as a social necessity, which would win the approval of Latitudinarians, there are cases (pathological we may think them, though they are not a few) who cannot find peace or personal integration by intellectual conviction or moral resolve or the assurance of external authority. They must go on pilgrimage to get rid of their burden and not to a town called Morality, which will lead them, though not everyone, to fearsome Mount Sinai, to the thunder and the quaking earth and the sound of the trumpet of doom. They need light, the light of the promises, which shines over the wicket-gate, the entrance to the pilgrim way of which the end is Mount Zion, the City of the Living God, the heavenly Jerusalem.

Bidden by Evangelist, for he cannot discover the way by himself or by private reading of Scripture without some human intermediary to point it out, the Man, soon to be known by his name of Christian, begins, in spite of his burden, to run towards the light. He runs away from his wife and children and stops his ears against their cries for him to return.

Robert Bridges regarded this as "a disastrous opening". It is a most selfish desertion, not on a par with Bunyan's own choice to go to prison and leave his wife and family in want, rather than compromise his principles. Christian leaves them to their fate in a city doomed to destruction. "That pious pagan Aeneas would have had them all on his back."[11]

On this three things need to be said, first that this is not necessarily physical but spiritual desertion, as Part II implies; Christian has gone on a spiritual journey and his wife and children are not willing to accompany him, indeed they call him back. Second, he does not cease to love them; he weeps for loss of them at Palace Beautiful, though admittedly this conversation with Charity is in the second edition. Third, in the end they follow his example; his influence, though not till after his death, induces them to go on pilgrimage as well.

In a fine passage Neil Keeble contrasts *The Pilgrim's Progress* at this point with Adam's unconditional surrender to his love of Eve in taking the apple from her in *Paradise Lost*. "The fidelity in *Paradise Lost* which is in fact ignoble though it appears noble, recognises, like the desertion in *The Pilgrim's Progress*, which is noble though it appears ignoble, that absolute devotion to any human being brings not blissful freedom but enslavement."[12]

The way to the wicket-gate

Obstinate and Pliable try to dissuade Christian but without success and Pliable, attracted by the promises of the glories of heaven, decides to accompany Christian; but immediately they find themselves in the Slow of Dispond, from which Pliable manages to extricate himself and slink home much aggrieved.

Christian sinks deeper into the mire because of his burden. The Slow is the invention of deep psychological insight again born out of Bunyan's own experience, the hazards of his own pilgrimage and his travels on country roads. Christian often sings on pilgrimage but his path is never one of sustained happiness. Until he is over the river at the last, his joy alternates with perils and anxieties. Help lifts him out of the Slow and sets him on his way again. The Dreamer asks Help why the place is not mended and is told that it cannot be even though the King has employed many labourers over sixteen hundred years who have poured "twenty thousand cart loads; yea Millions of wholesome Instructions, the best materials from all over the King's dominions"; but

> it is the Slow of Dispond still, the descent whither the scum and filth that attends conviction for sin doth continually run . . . for still as the sinner is awakened about his lost condition, there ariseth in his soul many fears, doubts and discouraging apprehensions, which all of them get together and settle in this place.

The steps, carefully laid by the Lawgiver, are quite concealed in bad weather.

Christian next meets Mr Worldly-Wiseman with the consequences we have mentioned. On his way to Morality, to the house of Legality, who it is said will painlessly remove his burden, he finds himself under Mount Sinai. Evangelist reappears and rebukes him severely with the word of God, so that he falls down trembling. Evangelist raises him to his feet again and exposes Mr Worldly-Wiseman as one who favours "only the Doctrine of the World", "for it saveth him from the Cross".

This is Bunyan's real condemnation of Latitudinarianism. There are echoes of Luther in it. Though he would not have borrowed the Latin on this occasion, his is a *Theologia crucis* not a *Theologia gloriae*. There is no Christianity without the cross, the cross that carries us and the cross that we carry.

Evangelist's stern words are corroborated by words and fire out of the mountain that make "the hair of poor Christian's flesh stand". The words were from Galatians 3:10, "as many as are of the works of the law are under the curse: for it is written, Cursed is every one that continueth not in all things which are written in the book of the law to do them".

Christian fears that there is no hope for him now, but Evangelist, while emphasising again the gravity of his sin – "thou hast forsaken the way that is good to travel in forbidden paths" – assures him that he will not be turned away from the wicket-gate . . . He parts from him with a kiss, gives him "one smile" ("the virile sweetness of this smile is one of the happiest inspirations of the book")[13] and bids him God speed.

Christian returns to the right road and when "in process of time" he reaches it he is accepted at the wicket-gate, though he needs to be pulled in because of the danger of death from the arrows of Beelzebub's castle. The Evil One intends that Christians will die before they are through the gate and truly on the way.

Good Will examines Christian on his past and assures him that none who comes is cast out – an echo of one of Bunyan's favourite texts, John 6:37, on which he preached his sermon "Come and welcome to Jesus Christ". He shows him the straight and narrow way, "cast up by Patriarchs, Prophets, Christ and his Apostles", and admits to many false paths adjoining, but recognisable being crooked and wide. But Good Will cannot remove Christian's burden, for the wicket-gate is not the place of deliverance.

Christian proceeds and soon comes to the Interpreters house where he is shown many things symbolic of salvation, like the pleading, pastoral preacher and the bonfire doused with water and replenished with oil, and the man in the iron cage shut in for ever because he, once of dedicated and religious life, has been seduced by wantonness and lust. And now he can find no place of repentance. The last had been Bunyan's own fear. The man in the cage is based on Francis Spira, whom Bunyan cites in *Grace Abounding, The Barren Fig-Tree, The Heavenly Footman* and *The Greatness of the Soul*. Despair was a component of seventeenth-century religion, not entirely due to religiously-induced guilt and fear, or to the Calvinist doctrine of election. Social factors, the conditions of life were also causes.

Bunyan thought he had found a way through, though Doubting Castle is still to come for Christian.[14]

There is a final sight of the man who had dreamed of the Apocalypse, that he was present on the day of Wrath, of Judgement, and terribly uncertain of his own fate. Christian leaves gratefully and soon finds his way fenced in by the Wall of Salvation. He runs but not without difficulty because of his burden.

At the cross

And then he arrives:

> at a place somewhat ascending; and upon that place stood a *Cross*, and a little below in the bottom, a Sepulcher. So I saw in my Dream, that just as *Christian* came up with the *Cross*, his burden loosed off from his Shoulders, and fell off from his back; and began to tumble; and so continued to do, till it came to the mouth of the Sepulcher, where it fell in, and I saw it no more.

He looks and wonders for "it was very surprizing to him that the sight of the Cross should thus ease him of his burden". It is the empty cross at which he gazes, but when he recounts the experience at Palace Beautiful he says that he saw "one, as I thought in my mind, hang bleeding upon the tree; and the very sight of him made my burden fall off my back". In western Catholicism and Latin America the crucifix, though sometimes the instrument of a diseased imagination, too oppressively prevalent and not wholly justified by the New Testament, is in some ways necessary to Christian devotion in that it shows the extent of Christ's identification with sufferers and the cost of the victory. "The old-rugged Cross" by itself may become a totem. It is not the wood which saves Christian. He sings:

> Blest Cross! blest Sepulcher! blest rather be
> The Man that there was put to shame for me.

It is important, taking up our comment on Mr Worldly-Wiseman's desire for a Christianity without the cross, that we recognise that the cross on which the Son of God offered himself once for all for our sins is the sign and instrument of our salvation, but it also points the way along which we must follow him. Bunyan is not as implicit about this in *The Pilgrim's Progress* as he is when he writes elsewhere:

> The cross is the standing way-mark by which all they that go to glory must pass by . . . Christ is the way . . . if thou art in him, thou wilt presently see the cross, thou must go close by it, thou must touch it, nay, thou must take it up, or else thou wilt quickly go out of the way that leads to heaven.[15]

The cross may be recognised in six things:

1 in justification by which we repudiate our own righteousness, our pious exercises and self-centred efforts to acquire virtue, and throw ourselves wholly on Christ;
2 in mortification, our death to self and "to the world and all its toys" (the phrase is Charles Wesley's);
3 in perseverance, a holding on to the end for all the thousands of miles of the journey, "briars and quagmires and all other incumbrances";
4 in self-denial;
5 in patience;
6 in giving to the poor, that ancient mark of Christianity, not in remote and detached benevolence but in communion and genuine fellowship with them.

Christian looks and weeps and as he does so the three shining ones appear and pronounce peace and forgiveness, reclothe him, seal him on his forehead with the seal of the Spirit and give him the sealed roll which is to be read on the way and is his passport to the Celestial City.

Hill Difficulty and Palace Beautiful

Christian goes on, fails to arouse Simple, Sloth and Presumption, has an argument with Formalist and Hypocrisy, who come tumbling over the wall on to the way and with whom he is stern and unrelenting since they have not come in "by the door".

There are no fewer than fifteen false pilgrims in *The Pilgrim's Progress* Part I, and Hypocrisy is what damns most of them. In our usage a hypocrite is one who misrepresents himself to others in an attempt to deceive. Robert Bolton called this "Grose" hypocrisy. But he also classified two other types. The formal hypocrite was one who had the appearance of a believer

81

but did not persevere, whose faith was but temporary; he deceived himself as well as others. But the "privie" hypocrite, ignorant of his own true state, who had no intent to deceive, but through inadvertency, carelessness or sloth, honestly believed himself to be better than he was. These two categories "would not by modern standards be considered hypocrites at all, since they were sincere in their representations to others. Bunyan's century was less forbearing than ours, since the mystery of election was at issue".[16]

Christian has no easy passage for he has to climb the Hill Difficulty which Formalist and Hypocrisy evade to their destruction, but which he has to ascend on his hands and knees. He rests in an arbor provided for pilgrims half-way up, but falls asleep, whereas he should have but taken a little ease. On resuming his climb he meets Timorous and Mistrust who frighten him with talk of lions ahead, looks for his roll for courage, discovers he has slept and has to retrace his steps instead of going forward. He finds his roll where he had lost it and goes on his way nimbly up the rest of the hill. But he has lost time, night has fallen and the lions will be abroad, so that although he sees the Palace Beautiful ahead he is fearful and especially when the lions appear, barring his entrance. The Porter of the Palace, who is within earshot, shouts that they are chained and there but for the trial of his faith.

He has to tell his story at the Palace to the young woman appropriately named Discretion and it is received with smiles and tears. Other maidens are summoned, Prudence, Piety and Charity, though the last does not speak in the first edition, and there is much talk and examination as in the fellowship of the gathered Church. It is interesting that the Palace is in charge of women, but there is no evidence elsewhere that Bunyan was particularly enlightened in this matter according to our modern standards.

Then there is Supper when "all their talk was about the lord of the Hill; as namely about what he had done and wherefore he did what he did and why he had builded that House". The implicit doctrine of Atonement is of "Christus Victor", though the battle was fought out of love. There is also testimony to the resurrection. "Some of them of the Household had said, they had seen and spoke with him since he did dye on the Cross". And, most significantly, it is all done for the poor. "He stript himself of his glory that he might do this for the Poor" and that they heard him say and affirm, that he would not dwell in the Mountain of *Zion* alone. After a night in a chamber called Peace Christian is shown the records, the histories of the saints, the willingness of the Lord to receive sinners, the equipment for service and for war, the relics and these not the inventions of medieval legend but all from Scripture, Moses' rod, Jael's hammer and nail, Gideon's pitchers, trumpets and lamps, Shamgar's goad, Samson's jaw-bone, David's sling and stone. And from the top of the house he sees the Delectable Mountains and Immanuel's Land, which is not enclosed nor the property of some earthly landlord with "keep out" notices and warnings that trespassers will be prosecuted, but is common to all pilgrims.

Meanwhile Faithful has passed by and gone on ahead.

Apollyon and the Two Valleys

The four girls, having accoutred Christian with armour, accompany him to the foot of the hill, for he is to descend into the Valley of Humiliation. They give him a viaticum of bread and wine and a cluster of raisins. And he needs it for at once he encounters Apollyon, a hideous monster, a hybrid, apocalyptic beast with scales like a fish, wings like a dragon, feet like a bear, "and out of his belly came Fire and Smoak, and his mouth was the mouth of a lion". Christian stands up to him, confronting him face to face. Apollyon wants to send him back to the country from which he has come. But Christian refuses and they fight. The combat has some reminiscences of that of George and the dragon. It lasts half a day, Christian is wounded and weak. Apollyon turns to wrestling, throws Christian, whose sword flies out of his hand, but just as the monster is about to strike the deadly blow he manages to reach out his hand and catch it and Apollyon is at his mercy. And this not so much because of the sword, but because of a word recalled from the prophet Micah, "Rejoice not against me, O mine enemy, when I fall, I shall arise." He also remembers Romans 8:37, "Nay, in all these things we are more than conquerors through him that loved us." The return of his courage due to his memory of Scripture gives him the victor's confidence. Christian wounds Apollyon severely and he spreads out his dragon's wings and speeds away. But it was a terrible fight with Apollyon's roars and Christian's groans.

Christian's wounds are healed by leaves from the tree of life which the hand of an invisible body supplies. He refreshes himself with the bread and wine which the girls from Palace Beautiful have given him.

An almost worse ordeal lies ahead. He must enter the Valley of the Shadow of Death and travel along a narrow way between a mire and a ditch. And in the middle of the valley, "hard-by the Wayside", is the mouth of hell. He has been walking with his sword drawn, but the sparks of hell force him to sheathe it and "betake him to another weapon called

All-Prayer". Fiends approach but he repulses them by crying out "I will walk in the strength of the Lord God". He no longer knows his own voice and thinks that the blasphemous whisperings of Satan's minions come from his own mind. And then, alone and disconsolate, he hears a man's voice, "Though I walk through the valley of the shadow of death I will fear none evil, for thou art with me." Then he knows that he is not alone and he hopes to have company by and by. The day breaks and he can see the hazards more clearly and although the second part of the valley is even more dangerous than the first, with "snares, traps, gins, nets and pits and deep holes", he now has light for his path.

And so he reaches the end of the valley with the grim sight of the bones and blood and ashes and mangled bodies of pilgrims who had perished there.

The companionship of Faithful

Christian now passes the cave where two giants, Pope and Pagan, used to live. Bunyan is unrealistic here. Pagan is far from dead three hundred years later and is both a mentor and a menace to Christianity. Pope cannot be written off as a gibbering and harmless geriatric. This was not true even when Bunyan wrote and since then there have been strong Popes capable of reforming the Church and taking a lead in the world, so that ecumenical discussions with Rome have to treat the question of primacy with great seriousness. Understood as the ARCIC Reports have defined it as a primacy of proclamation, of the unconditional love of Christ and of servanthood, it could be the hope of a united world Church, though ecumenism is now somewhat jaded and the centralism of Rome has, it is said, lost continents. But, for Bunyan, the papacy still meant Mary Tudor's Spanish burnings.

Christian climbs "a little ascent" which was cast up on purpose that pilgrims might have a view ahead, and from there he sees Faithful. He hails him but Faithful will not stay, so Christian runs and overtakes him, but in his eagerness and self-satisfaction stumbles and falls. Faithful helps him to his feet and they go "very lovingly on together".

They exchange accounts of their journey so far. Faithful tells of Pliable's sad state in the City of Destruction, ostracised as a turncoat by those who equally refused the pilgrim way; and he describes how Wanton, a Potiphar's wife, tried to seduce him, and an old man at the foot of Hill Difficulty tempted him with his service and attendant sensual pleasures until he discerns his identity written in his forehead and realises that this is the old man whom Scripture tells us to "put off" with his deeds. To have followed him would have been slavery. It is noteworthy that Faithful's temptations, unlike Christian's (and Bunyan's) are very much to sins of the flesh. This is why he was assailed by Moses, the angry, unmerciful Moses, not the meek, punishing every transgression of the law. Faithful is saved from him only by the intervention of the Lord Christ, recognised by the wounds of his passion. He passed by the Palace Beautiful to Christian's regret. He then encountered Discontent and Shame; the latter haunted him for a long time for he was half-ashamed to be socially ostracised and cast out of the company of "the great and the good" because of his religion. But for Faithfull the sun shone all the way through the valleys of Humiliation and the Shadow of Death.

After Christian has told his story they meet Talkative, who deceives Faithful, who sometimes might be called Credulous, but Christian knows him, the son of Saywell who lives in Prating Row. He is nothing but Talk. Faithful tests him with a long speech about the work of grace in the soul, almost as though there were a reversal of roles. Finding out that his religion is all words and not substance, Faithful denounces him and he departs indignantly.

After a trudge through a wilderness, beguiled by a conversation about their experiences, Evangelist overtakes them. His purpose is to warn them of the temptations of Vanity Fair, which they will soon enter and the trials which await them there – "one, or both of you, must seal the testimony which you hold with blood".

Vanity Fair

Vanity Fair is described in great detail and with no little satire.[17] It is the city of the world, not the secular city nor the industrial, nor the great twentieth-century conurbation, but the place of getting and spending, of international commerce, of fairgrounds and amusements and an under-world of crime. It is the city of the Restoration Court, of dubious financiers, corrupt magistrates, greedy prelates and petty thieves, licentious grandees and slum libertines. It is a crowded city, the city of the mob. It might be the ruin of an innocent country girl or of pilgrims spending their all on luxuries and bric-à-brac. It is the place where money rules as it had done in the Church of Rome with the sale of indulgences and pardons; the place which conformist religion tolerated and into whose business it entered.

Yet it is a place through which the road to the Celestial City runs, for pilgrims cannot escape the world.

These two men are in stark contrast to those at the fair. They are conspicuously different. Their clothes are not according to the fair's fashions, they speak "the language of Canaan", and to the question "What will ye buy?" they answer, "We buy the truth." They cause a hubbub and are taken for examination. They are beaten, besmeared with dirt and put into a cage as public spectacles and are mocked. But this causes further hubbub since there are those who think they are being unjustly treated. They are brought before the Examiners again as disturbers of the peace and further punished. They respond with such exemplary fortitude and patience that more are won over to them, and their enemies conclude that the only solution is to remove them by death. So they are arraigned before Lord Hategood, who may be modelled on Judge Kelynge who condemned Bunyan, though he sounds like the Judge Jeffreys of folklore, who in fact came a few years later. The trial is long, the witnesses false, the jury corrupt. It is reminiscent of the trial of Christ and of Foxe's martyrs. Faithful is sentenced to death and after cruel tortures is burnt at the stake. Christian escapes in a manner not described and resumes his pilgrimage.

Hopeful and various encounters

"Now I saw in my dream that Christian went not forth alone." Thus, movingly, Bunyan introduces Christian's new companion, Hopeful, converted by seeing Faithful and Christian at the fair. It is true to Christian experience that we are given new friends when the old are taken from us, which does not imply inconstancy or faithlessness but rather the inexhaustible communion of saints.

The first person Christian and Hopeful meet is Mr By-ends. The name means one who lives a respectable and religious life for his own advantage, not out of faith in God or as the overriding purpose of life. Religion is a by-product of self-interest and once it becomes costly and against the trend of the times, once it goes in rags and not silver slippers, they will abandon it. It is significant that By-ends has become "a Gentleman of good quality" though of humble origins. He is married to "my Lady Faining's daughter", but his great-grandfather was but a waterman "looking one way and rowing another". "And I got most of my estate by the same occupation."

As the gospels state so clearly, prosperity militates against true religion because it gives one a stake in the present age and, faith unless it buttresses the status quo, is socially disturbing and inimical to socially recognised values. By-ends is a biting satire on conformity. His conversation with his friends was added in the third edition of *The Pilgrim's Progress*. They and Mr Hold-the-World, Mr Moneylove and Mr Save-all, are pupils of Mr Gripe-man, "a schoolmaster in Love Gain which is a market town in the County of Coveting in the North". Is this a tilt at Scottish Presbyterianism?

By-ends and his companions defend the use of religion as a means to prosperity. It is not wrong for a minister to become more zealous and devoted in his work to secure a better benefice – he will become a better man in consequence of his more serious studies and greater dedication. A tradesman of modest means who turns to religion in order to marry a rich wife and gain better customers is promoting goodness in almost every sense of the term, economic as well as ethical.

When these arguments are put to Christian he dismisses them with contempt. "For if it be abominable to follow Christ for loaves, as it is in John 6, how much more abominable is it to make of him and his religion a stalking horse to get and enjoy the world."

Christian and Hopeful then cross the plain called Ease, which they are soon over since, says the margin, "Pilgrims have but little in this life". They then encounter Demas, again "gentleman-like", "over against the silver-mine", who invites them to turn aside to dig without too much sweat for treasure. Hopeful is minded to go but Christian knows Demas as the deserter of Paul, "his heart set on the present world" (2 Tim. 4:9) and gives him a dastardly pedigree – his great-grandfather Gehazi, his father Judas. By-ends and his companions accept Demas's offer and are seen no more.

The pilgrims then pass by a strange monument, Lot's wife turned into a pillar of salt for looking back to Sodom. This incident belongs to the second edition. It stands as a terrible warning that the divine judgement may strike not only those who wander from the pilgrim way but those who, while remaining in it, look back to the old life, its prizes and possessions.

Doubting Castle

They now spend some pleasant days on the banks of the river of the water of life, but once they depart, much refreshed, the river and the way separate, the way becomes hard, and, like the Israelites in the wilderness, they become much discouraged and turn into the alluring By-path meadow. It is Christian who persuades Hopeful that they should take it; but it leads to darkness and to the grounds of Giant Despair, who soon apprehends them and forces them to Doubting Castle where he puts them "in a very dark Dungeon, nasty and stinking to the spirit of these two men".

There intervenes the bedroom conversation between Giant Despair and his wife Diffidence, which again is an insertion in the second edition and a very human one. The giant is clearly under his wife's thumb. She is the more cruel and tells him to beat the prisoners, which he does, but they survive, though in great pain. Diffidence then tells the giant to invite them to make away with themselves by "Halter, knife or poison". Seeing their hesitation the giant would have killed them himself had he not been seized by one of his fits, to which he was prone in sunny weather and which paralyses his hand.

Thus spared though but half-alive, they debate whether to end their days. They are not made less dejected by a further visit from an enraged giant threatening the direst fate. Christian, swooning, thinks they should take the giant's advice, but Hopeful justified his name by reminding Christian of his past endurance and victories. The giant again asks his wife's advice and next morning takes them into the castle-yard and shows them the bones and skulls of former pilgrims. He does not kill them then and there but tells them that in ten days such will be their fate. They are to continue to live in Doubting Castle to prolong the agony of their hopelessness.

It is now Saturday, a day of great significance in the Christian calendar, as Bunyan surely must be aware, though he does not hold to a liturgical spirituality. It is the Saturday of impenetrable silence when the Lord lay in the tomb, the Saturday of the vigil of the resurrection, the "one particular day in western history about which neither historical record nor myth, nor Scripture make report. It is a Saturday and it has become the longest of days."[18] At midnight they begin to pray and continue almost to the break of day. Then Christian suddenly remembers that he has a key called promise which will open any door in Doubting Castle.[19] And so it proves even though the lock of the Iron Gate "went damnable hard" – Bunyan lapses into one of the expletives of his youth. The creaking gate awakens the giant, who started in pursuit, but being taken with one of his fits, they go free.

This is all true to Bunyan's own experience and, as already mentioned, to the state of many in his time. Bunyan believed that from infancy men and women should be made to feel depressed about their condition, yet for pilgrims despair is a sign that they have departed from the right way and ignored the promises. As he is to argue rhetorically in *Good News for the Vilest of Men*, "Despair! It is the devil's fellow, the Devil's master; yea the Chains with which he is captivated and held under darkness for ever."[20]

From the mountains to the river

And so they come to the Delectable Mountains, like Palace Beautiful a form of the Church, on which "there is no finer line in all literature" than that of the shepherds: "These Mountains are Immanuel's Land and they are within sight of the City, and the sheep also are his and he laid down his life for them." Once more they are shown "wonders", which bear warnings of danger, the hill Error, the mountain Caution, the By-way to hell for hypocrites. But they are also taken to the top of the hill clear, where they are given the "Perspective Glass" through which they may see the gate of the Celestial City. But their hands shake through remembering the terrible fate of hypocrites and they cannot look steadily through the glass; "yet they thought they saw something like the Gate, and also some of the Glory of the place".

They depart with warnings of hazards still to come. And they meet Ignorance.

Ignorance has been judged one of Bunyan's artistic failures. His fate is perplexingly severe. It almost dims the glories of the pilgrims' entry into the Celestial City. True he is brash and irritating, "a very brisk lad from the Country of Conceit". One has met him, a glib, self-assured talker, who does not really listen to other people's views but dismisses them with sneering condescension. But would Dante have consigned him to hell? And what of him, who, according to some witnesses, prayed for the ignorant as they crucified him? Ignorance represents some of the complexities of Bunyan's own life. He was dismissed by the establishment as ignorant and unfit to preach. He turns the tables by damning Ignorance who was in some ways, one fears, the epitome of Anglicanism as Bunyan saw it. And yet there is also a trace both of social rebellion against a system which would keep the vast majority of people ignorant and of the Puritan hatred of ignorance, both intellectual and, above all, spiritual, the inability to know God and that you are his child.

Isabel Rivers has rightly discerned that "It is important that Ignorance's account of his views follows Hopeful's detailed history of his conversion;

the juxtaposition of two rival creeds represents the most carefully worked out theological statement in *The Pilgrim's Progress*."[21]

Before that there is the story of Little-Faith, attacked and robbed of the money he had with him, though not of his real treasures, his jewels, that is, his saving faith. Therefore he is not excluded from the Celestial City. But he is so obsessed with the highway robbery and so full of complaints about his immediate loss that he forgets his real wealth, true of those Christians who moan about their losses and troubles by the way and ignore their heavenly treasure in Christ. Hopeful, who is sometimes rather shallow theologically, thinks that he might have pawned his jewels or sold them, as Esau his birthright. Christian dismisses this with tart superiority. There is no comparison between the two: Little-Faith has faith, even if it be only as a grain of mustard seed. He prizes his jewels too much to dispose of them for his immediate advantage. He may be pitied but not condemned.

He is the antithesis of Great-heart in Part II. But "all the King's subjects are not his Champions". And even these last must not be over-bold or swagger with confidence. The fight is hard, the warfare long. Great-Grace may bear grievous scars from combat with the minions of Satan. Yet Christian and Hopeful are soon in the Flatterer's net in spite of the Shepherds' warning. They are rescued by a Shining One with a whip in his hand who chastises them, though out of the love of God.

They next meet Atheist, "that boisterous renegade,"[22] who would laugh them out of the way. He has all the self-confidence, assurance of his own freedom from illusion and scorn for believers, of the person who has once believed, though not profoundly enough to withstand the seeming absence of God, or, in our own day, the obvious (and agonising) problems of nature and history. He deserves the answer of a modern saint to someone who said "I can't believe in God in the face of the choler microbe": "Don't be flippant!" Admittedly that is no easy answer and has the "scandal" of faith in it.

No sooner are they quit of Atheist than they enter the Enchanted Ground and Hopeful is overcome with drowsiness and is saved from fatal sleep by Christian, which makes him grateful for company, "Two are better than one." Christian's remedy for drowsiness is "to fall into good discourse" and so Hopeful tells of his conversion from indulgence in the life of Vanity Fair to the pilgrim way. It is the most succinct account of saving faith in all Bunyan's writings. Hopeful could not find peace simply through reformation of manners. These could not cancel his old debt of sin, even if he now paid "cash down" for everything. As a hymn of Charles Wesley's has it, "present for past can ne'er atone". And he also began to realise that

"All our righteousness is filthy rags", that it is not only our gross sins of which we need to repent and which afront God, but our holiest exercises and our most religious intentions.

It was Faithful who helped him to see that he needed another's righteousness to cover his own sin and thereby change him into the divine likeness. He must pray that God will reveal his Son in him. The prayer was not at first answered any more than for Bunyan himself. But in the depth of his sorrow for his sins he thought he saw the Lord Jesus look down from heaven and say, "Believe in the Lord Jesus Christ and thou shalt be saved." And Hopeful learned that "believing and coming were all one" and that the sheer longing for salvation in Christ is saving faith.

Here is the quintessence of Bunyan's theology. Here are the texts which meant most to him: "My grace is sufficient for thee" and "Him that cometh to me I will in no wise cast out".

This made Hopeful despondent about the natural state of the world. It also helped him to understand how the just God could accept sinners without denying his own nature – he gives them Christ to "put on". He became aware of his own ignorance and of what Samuel Rutherford called "the drawing loveliness of Christ":

> It made me love a holy life and long to do something for the Honour and Glory of the Name of the Lord Jesus. Yea, I thought, that had I now a thousand gallons of blood in my body, I would spill it all for the sake of the Lord Jesus.

Ignorance, in contrast, will never believe that his heart is as bad as the texts Christian adduces assert. He confesses his faith:

> I believe that Christ died for sinners, and I shall be justified before God from the curse, through his gracious acceptance of my obedience to his Law. Or thus, Christ makes my Duties that are Religious, acceptable to his Father by vertue of his Merits; and so shall I be justified.

This is legalistic, though it safeguards from Antinomianism. Christian is scathing and altogether condemnatory. Ignorance is sceptical of revelations, of specific experience, but insists that his faith is as good as the pilgrims', "though I have not in my head so many whimsies as you". He cannot understand what the pilgrims mean when they urge him to "flie to the Lord Jesus" and be saved by God's righteousness, not his own. Ultimately he believes that he will be saved or damned by works. Christian feels for him, "for it will certainly go hard with him at the last".

Ignorance is left behind and Christian discourses on fear of the Lord, which is the beginning of wisdom since it is caused by conviction of sin, drives the soul to Christ and keeps it in reverence for God and his word and the conscience tender. Christian talks of Temporary, who is for a while a pilgrim but apostasies, largely because all the while he is like a prisoner before a Judge, more afraid of the halter than of the offence committed. He traces the lapse into degeneration stage by stage.

This brings Christian and Hopeful out of the Enchanted Ground to Beulah Land where they are within sight of the City and meet some of the inhabitants. Bunyan uses the imagery of the Song of Songs, of the winter past, the flowers appearing in the earth and the voice of the turtle-dove heard in the land. Yet his desire for the City is such that Christian falls sick of love.

As they go on their way, they are met by two men, radiant in dress and faces, who say that there are but two difficulties more. The pilgrims ask the men to go with them, which they do, but they cannot be surrogates for the pilgrims' faith which must be their own.

And so they come to the river, which they had not known was between them and the gate; the river which is not a folk memory of Styx but the Jordan of Scripture.[23] And Christian, in particular, "began to dispond in his mind".

Entering the water he begins to sink straight away and cries out; but Hopeful seeks to cheer him for he feels the bottom. Yet Christian has another dark night to endure, "for he a great measure lost his senses" and can find no consolations. The thoughts of his sins weigh him down, he is troubled by apparitions of Hobgoblins and evil spirits. Such assurance as he had has gone. Hopeful bears him up and reminds him of the promises until Christian himself remembers Isaiah 43:2, "When thou passest through the waters, I will be with thee; and through the rivers, they shall not overflow thee." And so they find ground to stand on and the rest of the river is shallow. The shining ones await them and carry them up the high hill to the City which is above the clouds. And they talk of its glories in a passage of most poetic prose to describe the life of heaven. They will be with the patriarchs and receive reward for their toils and recompense for their woes. They will see the Holy One as he is and join in his endless praise. They will receive those who came after them and enjoy their friends again. They will also sit by the King of glory when he judges the wicked and have a voice in their sentence. They are greeted at the gate by a company of the heavenly host, and (in the second edition) by the King's trumpeters. Thus escorted they are "as 'twere in Heaven even before they come into it". When they come to the gate Enoch, Moses and Elijah are looking at them over it. They present their certificates and are admitted and as they enter they are transfigured. The dreamer has one glimpse of the City before the gates are shut again and like all who have a sight of those joys, he wishes himself among them. "Oh that we were there."[24]

And then comes Ignorance, after an easier passage than the pilgrims but with no certificate. His terrible fate shows that there is a way to hell even from the gates of heaven.

7

Three Later Books

The Life and Death of Mr Badman

In his Preface to *Mr Badman* (1680), Bunyan returns to the figure which he has used in his *Apology* for *The Pilgrims' Progress* Part I, the success of which prompted this work, and sees himself in the various guises of fisherman, fowler, archer, king's messenger and knight at arms. He has no doubt of the violence with which the book will apprehend the ungodly, or of the necessity of authorial heroics. He says that it will be "as impossible for this Book to go into several Families, and not to arrest some, as for the King's Messenger to rush into an house full of Traitors, and find none but honest men there"; and later, "*The man . . . that writeth* Mr Badmans life, *had need be fenced with a* Coat of Mail, *and with the Staffe of a Spear*." The atmosphere is that of the popish plot, "England shakes and totters already, by reason of the burden that Mr Badman and his friends have wickedly laid upon it."[1] The book also illustrates further the transition from the Bunyan who writes smartingly from his own experience to the Bunyan who is the objective observer of human nature. "To the best of my remembrance all the things that here I discourse of, I mean as to matter of fact, have been acted upon the stage of this world, even many times before mine eyes."

Mr Badman is clearly influenced by Arthur Dent's *The Plain Man's Pathway*. It is a dialogue between Mr Attentive and Mr Wiseman. It is a work of great craft and subtlety and, as Milo Kaufmann has shown, is really about God's providence and judgement of the wicked. Badman is through and through bad from his childhood. Lying was his signal though not his only fault. He was so:

addicted to lying that his parents could not distinguish when he was speaking the truth. He would invent, tell, and stand to the lies which he invented, with such an audacious face, that one might read in his very countenance the symptoms of a hard and desperate heart. It was not the fault of his parents; they were much dejected at the beginnings of their son, nor did he want counsel and correction, if that would have made him better: but all availed nothing.[2]

Attentive asks for instances of God's judgement on liars and Wiseman mentions Ananias (miscalled Saphira) and his wife from Acts 5:1ff. There are further fearsome anecdotes of God's judgement on swearers such as Dorothy Mately, a washer of rubbish at Derby lead mines. She stole twopence from the coat of a boy who was working beside her. When charged with the theft she wished the ground might swallow her if she had so much as touched his money. And soon afterwards the bank on which she was standing fell in and she was carried down with it, a stone fell on her head and she was buried in the rubble. When she was dug out, the money was found in her pocket. *But nothing like this happened to Badman.*

He was apprenticed to a man of sincere godliness who tried to reform him but his profligacy increased. A hard and wicked master followed and although conditions were harsh, "at least there was no godliness in the house which he hated worst of all". His father then set him up in business on his own, but his blackguard extravagance brings him almost to ruin. He sees a good marriage as the way out, so, not unlike the tradesman whom Mr By-ends's friend Moneylove has thought exemplary, he turns to religion to court a devout lady of independent means. On winning her, though she has been warned against him, he immediately returns to his wicked ways and adds to them the despicable and detested role of informer – under the Conventicle Acts – and threatens to denounce her minister. Mr Wiseman adduces lurid instances of the divine vengeance on all these miscreants from Hamor and Shechem to a hypocritical husband thrown from his horse, and informers at St Neots and Bedford given gangrene by a dog-bite or deprived of speech by a stroke. *But nothing like this happened to Badman.* Attentive is puzzled. "Certainly some wonderful judgement of God must attend and overtake such wicked men as these," he says. Wiseman replies, "You may be sure that they shall have judgement to the full, for all these things, when the day of judgement is come." There is a hint of "You just wait and see!" and that the reckoning may come with death.

Badman has his ups and downs. His wife bears him seven children, of whom one is gracious and good, three villainous and three a mixture of both parents. He prospers in business with the help of his wife's fortune but speculates and is nearly ruined a second time. He extricates himself by turning bankruptcy into a fine art. "He dealt by deceitful weights and measures" and in other nefarious ways. "To buy in the cheapest market and sell in the dearest" was his rule in business. Bunyan, the unlettered tinker, had a considerable knowledge of economics and condemns what has since become, in Froude's words, "a cardinal principle of wholesome trade".[3] Though it is an anachronism to put it in these terms, Bunyan was no monetarist and Mr Wiseman has a lengthy disquisition on the evil of "great gettings and abundance". The providence of God should overrule business dealings:

> If thou sellest do not commend. If thou buyest do not dispraise, any otherwise but to give the thing that thou hast to do with its just value and worth. Art thou a seller and things grow cheap? Set not thy hand to help or hold them up higher. Art thou a buyer and things grow dear? use no cunning or deceitful language to pull them down . . . If things rise do thou be grieved. Be also moderate in all thy sellings, and be sure let the poor have a pennyworth, and sell thy corn to those who are in necessity . . . [4]

Badman becomes very prosperous but there is partial judgement when one night, riding home drunk, his horse falls and he breaks his leg. In his pain and forced inactivity he becomes depressed and almost penitent, but his doctor says that his fears come "from an affection of the brain, caused by want of sleep" and are "nothing but vapours and the effects of his distemper" and he returns to his dissolute life. His wife, grieved by his relapse, dies of a broken heart. He plunges more than ever into debauchery and marries a prostitute to whom he has proposed under the influence of drink and with whom for sixteen years he lives a cat and dog life. They sin all his wealth away and when at last they part they are "poor as howlets".

Badman is not old, but (like the Stuart kings, we may think, and many at their court as well as in Bedford) his constitution has been undermined by his "cups and his queans". He has dropsy and gout and trouble in the bowels and, at the last, a consumption. Nothing has changed him. He is the selfsame Mr Badman to the end with no sign of remorse or repentance. And "he died like a lamb, or, as men call it, a chrisom child, quietly and without fear". For Bunyan, this is the sure sign of his damnation.

Judgement is judgement though it be concealed from any but those who believe in a just God, evidence or no. This is not convincing at first sight and may meet the riposte that Christians ridiculously maintain their faith in defiance of all logic. They look for God at work in events, sometimes by a misunderstanding of his nature as the more liberal Christianity proclaims it, but if he seems to be inactive in human affairs, he is still God and somehow his will ultimately prevails. This seems naïve and pathetic nonsense and far more tolerant of God, if there be a God, than he deserves. But Milo Kaufmann unveils the clue to the Puritan belief in Providence:

> The ability to discern providence which (Wiseman) and Attentive share, but which Badman so grievously lacks, is in fact the divine gift of an ordering faith. The ambiguity is never wrung out of events. The discernment of judgements moves from will to event, rather than from event to will. One exercises the will of the elect in so reading events; nothing in events coerces him. On the penultimate page of the narrative Wiseman determines the bedrock of the matter: "only the godly that are in the world have a sanctuary to go to, where the oracle and Word of God is, by which his judgements and a reason of many of them are made known to, and understood by them".[5]

Only when David went into the sanctuary of God did he see the reality of the divine judgement on the wicked (Psalm 73:17). Communion with God is the revelation, "but not without great painfulness . . . so deep so hard and so difficult did he find it, rightly to come to a determination in this matter". It is a great mystery and there are no glib interpretations. Only the deep, personal knowledge of God in the bottom of our hearts, not the top of our minds, brings us within sight of the answer, and then, we may add, under the shadow of a cross.

The Holy War

Bunyan is much more confident in his verse Apology for *the Holy War* (1682) than he was when he nervously and after much delay allowed *The Pilgrim's Progress* to be published. He is assured of the success of his method. Allegory is popular. There may also be "a softening rigour", in Milo Kaufmann's phrase.[6] The narrator finds the Continent of Universe "large and spacious . . . well watered and richly adorned with Hills and Valleys" while the City of Mansoul is an enviable place in which he would have stayed had he not been called to higher things. It is surely the prototype of the Puritan community, the body politic before the fall and therefore paradisal (*pace* Kaufmann). It is also the individual human being seen as a city with five impregnable gates "such as never be opened nor forced but by the will and leave of those within. The names of the gates were these:

Ear-gate, Eye-gate, Mouth-gate, Nose-gate, and Feel-gate. The genius of the allegory is in the fact that Bunyan so fully understands the relation between the individual and society. *The Holy War* is Bunyan's *Paradise Lost* and *Paradise Regained*. It is the story of the Fall and of the redemption through Christ, which is yet incomplete. If it is unsatisfactory as a work of art, this is because it deals realistically with human life as it is still, at the end of the second millenium of the so-called Christian era.

The founder and builder of Mansoul and its rightful king is Shaddai, though he does not live there. The leading citizens are the faculties of the human being. The Lord Mayor is Lord Understanding, the Recorder Mr Conscience, and Lord Willbewill as high born as any, with Mr Affection his deputy and Mr Mind his clerk.

The city is menaced by the giant Diabolus, "king of the blacks", a piece of lamentable racism by Christian standards today, but which may be overlooked in interpreting the allegory. He dresses like a snake (shades of Eden!) and the city falls to him with surprising ease – Captain Resistance is shot dead on the walls – and he proceeds to degrade the principle officers. Lord Understanding loses his position and is confined to his palace in front of which a wall is built to shut out the light, "so that till Mansoul was delivered the old Lord Mayor was rather an impediment than an advantage to that famous town". Conscience, the Recorder, one of Bunyan's many senior citizens, is much corrupted but not entirely debauched and every now and then remembers Shaddai, the city's rightful ruler and cries out loud enough to shake the whole town, his words like thunderclaps, which enables Diabolus to persuade the people that he is mad. He also makes him deny when he is "merry" what he has at times so stridently affirmed. Lord Willbewill has gone over entirely to the enemy and is made Captain of the Castle, Governor of the Wall and Keeper of the Gates. Affection becomes "vile" and Mind has a daughter named Carnal Lust. The succeeding officials are an evil crew representing the worst and most callous vices. Mr Lustings is Mayor and Mr Forget-Good Recorder. And of the burgesses and aldermen, Mr Incredulity is the eldest and Mr Atheist the youngest of the company.

News reached Shaddai of the capture of Mansoul. The court is dismayed, while in private the king and his son, Emmanuel, resolve to deliver Mansoul. The Lord Chief Secretary draws up a summary of the decision:

Let all men know who are concerned, that the Son of Shaddai, the great King is engaged by covenant to his Father to bring his Mansoul to him again; yea, and to put Mansoul, too, through the power of his matchless love, into a far better and more happy condition than it was in before it was taken by Diabolus.

When Diabolus hears this he keeps it from the citizens, though he warns them against the evil designs of Shaddai, arms them, and seeks so to promote wickedness and vice by allowing unrestrained appetites that in spite of the covenant Shaddai and his holy son will cast them off.

Shaddai does not yet send his son to Mansoul, though he sends fifty thousand soldiers under four captains – Boanerges, Conviction, Judgement and Execution – to the gates of Mansoul. They represent the Covenant of Works and will not be able to recapture the town, as Shaddai well knows. And so Emanuel himself, who has already offered the sacrifice to redeem Mansoul, comes to take command, clad in shining armour, with his chosen captains Credence and Good Hope, Charity, and Innocence and Patience and their squires Promise and Expectation, Pitiful, Harmless and Suffer Long. Emanuel's army has forty-four battering rams and twenty-two slings – the sixty-six books of the Bible – each of pure gold. Preparations are made for a siege, trenches are dug and mounds are thrown up. Diabolus parleys. He wants a compromise, to administer part of Mansoul under Emanuel, or at least live there or, failing that, to keep in contact with his friends and relatives. Emanuel will have none of it. There is battle beneath the walls and Emanuel's host is not unscathed but has the better of it. Diabolus again makes proposals, this time to establish a religious and Christian system, which, says Froude, "obviously means the Established Church".[7] This is the covenant of works in its most alluring aspect – the Church of England. Emanuel is outraged. Mansoul will be totally renewed, pulled down and built up again "as though it had not been, and it shall be the glory of the whole universe".

There is a second battle. Emanuel's army gains entrance through Eargate and makes its headquarters at old Recorder Conscience's house. There is terror in all hearts. Diabolus, who has retreated into the castle, comes out at last and surrenders. He cannot be made away with altogether but is stripped of his armour, bound to Emanuel's chariot wheels and ejected "into parched places in a salt land, where he might seek rest and find none".

Meanwhile Emanuel is disconcertingly silent over the fate of the townspeople. Prayers for mercy are seemingly ignored and a petition taken by Mr Desires Awake with a rope around his neck, since Captain Conviction will not be their advocate, is received by Emanuel with tears but he needs time to consider it. The former leaders, Understanding, Conscience and

WillbeWill, expect death any moment. They compile a confession of their misdeeds. They think of sending this by Old Good Deed, but fear that he will be rebuffed and told to save Mansoul himself. So Desires Awake goes again, still with a rope around his neck and Mr Wet Eyes accompanies him. Still Emanuel gives no comfort.

Next day the three prisoners must go themselves to the prince in his camp and they proceed, chained and guarded by soldiers "in drooping spirits". "Or, more particularly thus: the prisoners went down all in mourning: they put ropes upon themselves; they went on smiting themselves on the breasts, but durst not lift their eyes to heaven." When they reach the camp the sight and glory of the prince's army greatly heightens their affliction. They prostrate themselves before the glorious majesty, who puts them through a distressing examination until they confess that they have no excuse and are deserving of nothing but "death and the deep".

Emanuel's response is astonishing. The prisoners are left grovelling but there is an immediate proclamation of the divine victory and music resounds throughout the camp. There is joy everywhere except in the hearts of the men of Mansoul. And then the trembling prisoners are made to stand again before the prince and he declares a free and total pardon, strips them of their mourning weeds and gives them beauty for ashes, the oil of joy for mourning and the garment of praise for the spirit of heaviness. They "fainted almost quite away"; Lord WillbeWill "swooned outright; but the Prince stepped to him, put his everlasting arms under him, embraced him, kissed him, and bid him be of good cheer, for all should be performed according to his word". Similarly "he did kiss, and embrace, and smile upon the other two."

Emanuel enters the town in triumph as the bells ring and boughs and flowers are strewn in his path. The streets and squares are rebuilt. Lord WillbeWill resumes charge of the gates, Mr Understanding is reinstated as Lord Mayor, Mr Knowledge is made Recorder "not out of contempt for old Conscience, who was bye-and-bye to have another employment". Diabolus's image is taken down and hewn in pieces and joy is everywhere, with a great feast, food from Shaddai's court and the music of the masters of his songs.

There are, however, to be trials of Diabolus's servants. These are well described and the characters portrayed with great skill. They are unanimously found guilty and sentenced to be executed next day. Incredulity escapes in the night. The rest are crucified. One shudders to read it, until one remembers Paul's words about the need for our sins to be crucified; but they struggle desperately to avoid being nailed.

Mansoul is given a charter of rights. The government is to be in the hands of the Lord Chief Secretary of Shaddai's court and the old Recorder, Mr Conscience. He must confine himself to the teaching of virtue, of morality and duty, but must not attempt to presume to be a revealer of those high mysteries which the Chief Secretary, the Holy Spirit, alone can declare. Conscience is old and has been much abused and needs the constant refreshment, strengthening and purifying of the new wine of the kingdom. He is in the Christian life subordinate to the gospel. He warns the unconverted of the wrath to come, but he may torture through the proliferation of scruples, or deceive through assurances which simply have not reckoned with the sinfulness of sin. He may also become hardened; he needs above all to be kept tender, especially in believers, who are not yet content to rest in his approval but to the end cast themselves on the mercy of Christ.

This, however, cannot be the end of the Holy War. Diabolians – named after St Paul's list of vices in Colossians 3:5 – lurk outside the walls. Gradually the lusts of the flesh gain control again. Mr Carnal Security becomes eminent, the Chief Secretary is ignored. Conscience finds Knowledge and Lord WillbeWill dining with Carnal Security in his parlour. At last Diabolus is invited to return, to the delight of Hell. After some discussion as to timetable, Diabolus, who is impatient, raises an army of Doubters "from the land of Doubting on the confines of Hell Gate Hill". The inhabitants of Mansoul now realise what peril threatens and repent, killing such Diabolians as they are able to hunt out. But the terrible army advances, led by Incredulity who had escaped. The Chief Secretary will not help because he has been "grieved". The townsmen go out to meet the Doubters, singing Pslams.

In *The Holy War* Bunyan recalls much of what he must have seen and heard of armies in the Civil War almost forty years earlier. But after getting the better of an initial battle the townsmen are routed when, over confident, they attempt an attack at night when the Doubters are strongest. Once more the Diabolians storm the walls and enter the town and capture all except the castle. The state of Mansoul is worse than it has ever been. It becomes "a den of dragons, an emblem of Hell, a place of total darkness". Mr Conscience, hit near the heart in the first engagement, gets no rest through his festering wounds. Doubters are everywhere, rampaging and swearing as victorious soldiers sometimes do, though Froude thinks it a picture of fashionable London at the time.[8] The castle still holds out and the garrison sends a petition to Shaddai's court which the Lord Secretary has drawn up and signed. Otherwise it would not be received. Meanwhile the Doubters plot to reduce the castle by an ingenious scheme devised by

Lucifer, to make commerce dominate all and the pursuit of wealth be the main interest of the citizens. There will be such abundance of goods that the castle will become a warehouse and Diabolus's gang gain easy entrance.

Before this can happen the prince's forces appear, though without him at first. The town leaders rally, Captain Credence, still suffering from wounds, appears on crutches to the enemy's consternation, the troops engage with the cry "The sword of Emanuel and of Captain Credence" (shades both of Gideon and the New Model Army); but the battle is indecisive until the prince himself appears. Then there is victory and the trial of the enemy chiefs. The story ends with long speeches from Emanuel because still the victory is not total, still Diabolus is at large, still Carnal Security, escaped from prison, lurks in town, and Unbelief "they can never lay hold of".

This is a great mystery. Says Emanuel:

> Nothing can hurt thee but sin; nothing can grieve me but sin; nothing can make thee base before thy foes but sin; take heed of sin, my Mansoul. And dost thou know why I at first, and do still suffer Diabolonians to dwell in thy walls, O Mansoul? It is to keep thee wakening, to try thy love, to make thee watchful, and to cause thee yet to prize my noble captains, their Souldiers, and my mercy. It is also that yet thou maiest be made to remember what a deplorable condition thou once wast in. I mean when, not some, but all did dwell, not in thy walls, but in thy castle, and in thy stronghold, O Mansoul!

Were the city of the soul completely free from its enemies, it might be so much off guard as to let in the whole host from outside. The enemies may do the soul good if they keep it watchful and warring and drive it nearer to God for strength and reliance on him and not on its own resources:

> . . . let the sight of a Diabolian heighten thy love to me. I came once, and twice, and thrice, to save thee from the poyson of those arrows that would have wrought thy death: stand for me, thy friend, my Mansoul, against the Diabolians, and I will stand for thee before my Father, and all his court. Love me against temptation, and I will love thee notwithstanding thine infirmities.[9]

The other great theme is that of the relation of the faculties of the human soul to the divine powers, the Holy Spirit, grace and faith. They are indeed powerless without agencies of the gospel. We have already noticed the limits of the role of Conscience, his subordination to the Lord Secretary, the Spirit, while Emanuel rejects all petitions from Mansoul except that drawn up by the Lord Secretary, although the human faculties are not simply passive. Says the Lord Secretary, "True the hand and pen shall be mine, but the ink and paper must be yours, else how can you say it is your petition?[10]

It is a pertinent theme still. Emanuel in his final speech claims all the credit for himself:

> Nor did thy goodness fetch me again unto thee, after that I for thy
> transgressions have hid my face, and withdrawn my presence from
> thee. The way of backsliding was thine, but the way and means of thy
> recovery was mine. I invented the means of thy return . . . It was I
> that set Mr Godly-fear to work in Mansoul. It was I that stirred up
> thy conscience and understanding, thy will and thy affections, after
> thy great and woful decay. It was I that put life into thee, O Mansoul,
> to seek me, that thou mightest find me, and in thy finding find thine
> own health, happiness and salvation.[11]

This baffles the humanists and indeed some Christians as it did Bunyan's theological opponents. A psychoanalyst friend of mine is puzzled because he says that I attribute all my faults and failures to myself and any goodness to God. The fear of taking credit for any triumph of grace over sin for any achievement in the way of holiness is that it may lead to improper pride and complacency and also arise from ignorance of that self which is still unregenerate. And how can I judge? The actions which I deem good may not always be to the glory of God or to the true well-being of my neighbour. Better to live and act by faith and in total dependence on divine Grace, to say as in Harriet Auber's hymn on the Holy Spirit:

> And every virtue we possess
> And every conquest won
> And every thought of holiness
> Are his alone.

The Pilgrim's Progress Part II

Bunyan wrote Part II of *The Pilgrims Progress* (1684) partly in answer to popular demand, partly to pre-empt imitators. Some have considered it vastly inferior to Part I. Froude, for instance, regarded it as "but a feeble reverberation".[12] This I would dispute; but it is different. Milo Kaufmann is near the mark when he writes: "While in the first part Bunyan is concerned to disturb the comfortable, ensuring a close examination of the reader's own calling, in the second part his concern is plainly to comfort the disturbed."[13] John Stachniewski says: "Part Two as a whole is an expression of pride in the achievement of Christian, a path-breaking dissenter whose fugitive energy has succeeded in opening a psycho-social space for the next generation to inhabit. His offspring tread with collective assurance in his pioneering steps." He also finds "the mollifying of doctrine to consort with Bunyan's more comfortable position as pastor and parent".[14]

It does emanate from a more secure background, in spite of the suspicions and antagonisms and intermittent fears of the last years of Charles II's reign. The Nonconformists knew that they could not now be ousted from the life of England. They had their churches and *The Pilgrim's Progress* Part II could be seen as a picture of one of them. They feast to music and sing often on the way, hymns and songs and psalms are not prohibited in this congregation. At House Beautiful Christiana and Mercie hear music. And Mercie cries, "Wonderful! Musick in the House, Musick in the Heart, and Musick also in Heaven for joy that we are here."

Christian's wife's conversion is a result of his death – confirming the view that the separation of his pilgrimage has been spiritual rather than physical.

Christiana has no burden and nothing like her husband's or Bunyan's struggle with fear. She regrets the way she treated Christian, she has a bad dream which turns into a good one, and she receives a visit from Secret, who pronounces God's pardon and her acceptance at the Lord's table and offers her a perfumed letter written in gold, an invitation from the king himself to live in his city. The beatified Christian himself is showing anxious interest from on high, almost as though Bunyan was on the verge of the Catholic belief in the efficacy of the prayers of the departed saints. Christiana wants to be transported to heaven at once, but the visitor warns her that "the bitter is before the sweet". Her neighbours think she is foolish. Mrs Timorous, daughter of the man who met Christian on the Hill Difficulty and warned him of the lions, has most to say. But her resolve is unshaken and she departs with her four sons and Mercie, a gentle girl who leaves in tears at the thought of the fate of her impenitent relatives. The Slow is worse than formerly but they negotiate the steps successfully, though Christiana wobbles once or twice. She has to knock several times at the wicket-gate and is kept waiting while a vicious mastiff comes "barking upon them". The margin explains that the dog is the Devil, an enemy to prayer. A more vehement knocking gains admission, but Mercie faints outside for she has not received the king's invitation, only Christiana's. This does not matter; "I pray for all them that believe on me by what means soever they come." Later she is said to have knocked even harder and more desperately than Christiana.

They are received with the kiss of peace and pardon, instructed with glad words and shown Christ crucified afar off, the deed by which they are saved.

We will not follow them in detail as they travel Christian's road. They are nearly ravished by two ill-favoured men, which shows their need for a protector and one is given them as they leave the Interpreter's House, Great-heart, armed with sword and helmet and shield. They have seen many fresh emblems there including the man with the muckrake who was so intent on raking the straws and small sticks and dust of the floor that he did not look up to see one with a celestial crown in his hand.

Great-heart is leader, defender and giant-killer, but his first task is as theological counsellor. As they pause and bless God at the place where Christian's burden fell-off, Christiana asks Great-heart what is meant by "pardon by deed". "Pardon by word" she understands, but this puzzles her. He explains that this means that the pardon bestowed is not obtained by the person pardoned but is the work of another. "He has performed Righteousness to cover you, and spilt blood to wash you in." This makes Christiana ask what Righteousness the Redeemer will have for himself if he has parted with it to us, and leads Great-heart to discourse on the various aspects of Christ's righteousness, as God, as Man and in union of the two natures; and these he cannot give away else he would denude himself. But there is yet another righteousness which consists in his obedience to a revealed Will. And it is this which is his justifying gift to sinners. This is stiff evangelical scholasticism, alien to our methods of ratiocination, but in the end the individual appropriates the Church's praise of divine love in the great tradition of affective piety. Christiana says:

True; methinks it makes my Heart bleed to think that he should bleed for me. Oh! thou loving One. Oh! thou blessed One, thou deservest to have me; thou hast bought me: thou deservest to have me all; thou hast paid for me in ten thousand times more than I am worth! No marvel that this made the water stand in my Husbands Eyes, and that it made him trudge so nimbly on.

Great-heart raises the question whether the warmth of these affections will always be sustained and he points out that they are the communications of an especial grace. Not every one who has seen Jesus bleed has become his disciple. Some laughed at him and hardened their hearts. "So that all that you have, my Daughters, you have by a peculiar impression made by a Divine contemplating upon what I have spoken to you."

Great-heart slays Grim, or Bloody-man, back-up to the lions and representative of voracious and unjust landlords, among others. He blocks the King's Highway as some did the roads of England by enclosure. Great-heart has little trouble with him. They had hoped that Great-heart would be with them to the end but he leaves them at the Palace Beautiful for they have not asked that he should escort them further. They are shown more emblems and Mercie is courted by a visitor, Mr Brisk, well-bred and with some pretence to religion, but worldly. He has no sympathy with her making clothes for the poor and may be repelled by her explaining herself in "the language of Canaan". Even her alluring countenance cannot overcome his antipathy to her good words for the deprived. He ceases to call on her and gives as reason: "That Mercie was a pretty lass; but troubled with ill conditions." This is another indication that Bunyan is writing, not out of the hazards and uncertainties of prison but from the local church, where the interests are human and not simply in theological dialectic; and the account of Christiana giving medicine to her naughty boys is certainly from life, and not without humour even though the purges and pills have biblical reference. The stronger purge is made *ex carne et sanguis Christi* ("You know Physicians give strange Medicines to their Patients"): This physic is universal, good against all diseases to which pilgrims are prone. Christiana has twelve boxes of the pills; but they must always be taken "in half a quarter of a Pint of Tears of repentance".

As they are about to leave the Palace Beautiful, Great-heart returns, to their great delight. He brings a bottle of wine from his lord and some parched corn and two pomegranates for Christiana and Mercie and figs and raisins for the boys. On they go retracing the path of Christian, recalling his adventures and turning the topography to their edification. The Valley of Humiliation is not a place of conflict and peril. Christian was unfortunate enough to meet with Apollyon there, but it is normally a place of solitude, free from noise and danger where pilgrims are not "let and hindered" in their contemplation and where our Lord, in a moving reference to the incarnation, "formerly had his country house and loved much to be there". The Valley of the Shadow of Death is dark and terrifying with its stinks and smells and gins and snares, but with the help of Great-heart they are nearly through when Giant Maull confronts them and charges Great-heart with being a kidnapper of women and children, a charge which may well be laid against some religious adherents. The fight is fierce and long and Great-heart is forced down upon his knees at one stage and his skull nearly broken at another; but he prevails, when he pierces the giant under his fifth rib. He has conquered through remembering his Master, who was also brought to the ground.

On the journey they acquire more pilgrims and become a caravan. Some of Bunyan's best-known characters appear. Old Honest, from the town of Stupidity, is first. He discusses Mr Fearing, a pilgrim with whom he had travelled, and there is a fine account, deep in psychological understanding. "He had, I think, a Slow of Dispond in his mind, a Slow that he carried everywhere with him else he would never have been as he was." He was not afraid of external menaces like the Hill Difficulty or the lions. "For you must know that his Trouble *was not about such things as those*, his fear was about his acceptance at the last." Like Archbishop Leighton, his contemporary, Bunyan recognises that some by temperament walk in a covert, cloudy day, or as Great-heart says, play constantly upon the "Base". This is "the ground of Musick. And for my part, I care not at all for that Profession that begins not in heaviness of Mind."

Mr Feeble-mind is rescued from Giant Slaygood, another of Great-heart's victims. They will not leave him behind for it is Great-heart's commission to comfort the feeble-minded (1 Thess. 5:14) and they will deny themselves some things, "both Opinionate and Practical" for his sake. "We will not enter into doubtful Disputations before you, we will be made all things to you, rather than you shall be left behind." Mr Ready-to-Hault on crutches joins them and brings up the rear with Mr Feeble-mind. Mr Dispondencie, cadaverous with starvation and his daughter Much-afraid are found just about alive among the bodies in Doubting Castle. At the place where Little-Faith was robbed they find Mr Valiant-for-Truth bloody from a three-hour combat with Wild-head, Inconsiderate and Pragmatick, whom he has put to flight. It is he who sings the Pilgrims' hymn, "Who would true valour see". In the Enchanted Ground they find Standfast on his knees because he has been tempted by Madam Bubble, the vain world, the witch by whose sorceries the ground is enchanted.

They find Vanity Fair somewhat reformed. Faithful was its last martyr and in some parts of the town "Religion is counted honourable", an indication of somewhat easier conditions for Nonconformists in 1684. When they reach Doubting Castle Greatheart overcomes contrary opinions and takes Honest, and Christiana's four sons, now grown men, to attack the giant and demolish the castle. This they do. The giant is formidable in a cap of steel, a breastplate of fire, iron shoes and with a club in his hand. His wife, Diffidence, is cut down at one blow of Mr Honest, but the giant has as many lives as a cat and the fight is hard. Great-heart heaves and strikes until his head is severed. Then the castle is demolished.

It cannot be said that Despair was conquered easily; yet this second company of pilgrims did not succumb as Christian and Hopeful. There are two reasons for this. They were not trespassers, as were the two. Stachniewski has pointed out that:

> while on a literal level trespass is a specific crime against property it is also a near biblical synonym for sin; to be exact the Greek word for trespass in the New Testament means, aptly for Bunyan's allegory, "falling aside" . . . The laws of trespass were unforgiving as were the landowners who brought the prosecutions and the judiciary, dominated by them, which implemented sentences (justifiably simplified in the allegory into a single oppressor).[15]

Christian and Hopeful had transgressed the law and must be confined under the giant's harsh regime until Grace delivers them and for days they forgot its efficacy.

Secondly these pilgrims of Part II had Great-heart. He is resolute to kill the giant. It is the Pastor in the fellowship of the Church who may, though only after a long fight, kill Despair and decimate his dungeons.

It seems to be a longer, less rapid journey than Christian's, if not quite, as Ronald Knox has said, "a walking tour". There are inns and hospitable homes like those of Gaius and Mnason – names of persons briefly mentioned in the New Testament. Gaius is described in Romans 16:23 as "the host of himself and of the whole Church"; Mnason in Acts 21:16 as "of Cyprus, an old disciple with whom we should lodge". Here there are feasts with symbolic food and drink and much merriment, riddles are told and marriages made, notably Mercie to Christiana's Matthew. And there is music all the time.

They come at last to Beulah Land where the sun shines night and day and they wait in peace and fragrance for "the good Hour". There is to be no Gerontius-like revulsion from the sight of God, no Purgatory. The messenger comes first for Christiana and she takes leisurely farewell of her companions, praise and thanksgiving mixed with admonition. She is accompanied to the riverside, a foreshadowing of evangelical deathbed scenes in which death is not so much the last enemy as the first friend.

They all have plenty of time to prepare and none come near to sinking like Christian. Mr Dispondencie's daughter, Much-afraid, goes through the river singing, "but none could tell what she said".

Mr Valiant-for-Truth's crossing is still often read at the funerals of public figures, whether Christians or not. In these descriptions Bunyan's prose is at its most majestic with its reverberating beauties. Mr Standfast has the easiest passage of all. His final words of a calm death and the joy set before him speak the hopes of all those who believe as Bunyan did:

> This River has been a Terror to many: yea, the thoughts of it have also often frightened me. Now, methinks, I stand easie; my Foot is fixed upon that upon which the feet of the Priests that bare the Ark of the Covenant stood, while Israel went over this Jordan. The Waters indeed are to the Palate bitter, and to the Stomack cold; yet the thoughts of what I am going to, and of the conduct that waits me on the other side, doth lie as a glowing Coal at my Heart. I see myself now at the end of my Journey: my toilsome days are ended. I am going to see that Head that was Crowned with Thorns, and that Face that was spit upon for me. I have formerly lived by hearsay and Faith; but now I go where I shall live by sight, and shall be with him in whose Company I delight myself.

8
The Last Years

At the end of *The Pilgrim's Progress* Part II, Bunyan hints that it may be his lot "to go that way again" and give an account of what he has not told, presumably about Christiana's children and their families. But there is no Part III. He was not to have time, for his life ended earlier than might have been expected. The lack of Part III may be no great loss, for it is hard to think that (though Part II is as good a sequel as *Alice Through the Looking Glass* is to *Alice in Wonderland*, a comparison made by Gordon Rupp) the original inspiration could have been further sustained.

Bunyan was still engaged in controversies in the 1680s. In 1683 he published *A Case of Conscience Resolved*, in which he argues against women's meetings in church apart from men. It is a rejoinder to a paper from a "Mr K", thought to be William Kiffin of London, who had written in support of such meetings, of which Bunyan had persuaded the women of his Bedford congregation to "let go". Bunyan can find no support for separate gatherings for women in Scripture and one influential reason for his opposition was that such meetings smacked of the customs of Ranters and Quakers, which he regarded as inimical to the gospel; they are also "nunnish". He claims that women and men are spiritually equal. But we must conclude that in spite of their presiding presence in House Beautiful and his obvious interest in their pilgrimage in Part II of *The Pilgrim's Progress*, and the evidence of some understanding of female psychology in the whole work, he was somewhat shy of women in his personal relationships. He went so far as to say in self-defence in *Grace Abounding*, "It is a rare thing to see me carry it pleasant with a woman . . . Their company alone, I cannot away with. I seldom so much as touch a Woman's Hand." Salutations, that is, social kisses, which some pastors, who obviously enjoyed them, justified as "holy" kisses, he much deplored, and shrewdly noted that they were usually given to the most attractive women. Yet we must not ignore the earlier benefit received from the poor women of the

Bedford congregation. He makes the familiar protest, by no means confined to Puritans, against provocative dress, bare shoulders and breasts. In
his posthumously published *Exposition on . . . Genesis* he refers to women
as "that simple and weak sex". He was no apostle of their liberation and
while he admired and warmed to the Mercies, he would be capable of
telling jokes about henpecked husbands, for example Giant Despair, and
feel threatened by women's power and independence in the Church. Their
role was to be "resigned, submissive, meek", at any rate in public.[1]

In 1685 in *Questions About the Nature and Perpetuity of the Seventh-Day-
Sabbath* Bunyan attacks the Seventh-Day Baptists who believed that the
law to keep holy the seventh day, which pre-dated Sinai, was still binding
on Christians – this after all was what Christ himself had observed – and
that the first-day Sabbath was a Roman apostasy. These Baptists were
never a majority but they were represented throughout the counties, from
Lincolnshire to Dorset, and in three congregations in London. They often
combined their sabbatarian views with Millenarianism and Fifth-Monarchism. Like Richard Baxter and John Owen, Bunyan opposed them. He
had preached to the Congregationalist Church which shared Pinners Hall
in Broad Street, London with the Seventh-Day Baptists of Francis Bampfield, who was their outstanding apologist.

It is interesting that he is more "liberal" than Baxter, Owen and many
others who insist on the principle of "one day in seven". He is rather of
the spirit of the Reformer William Tyndale, who in his controversy with
Sir Thomas More asserted that, as Christians, we are lords of the Sabbath
and could make it any day we chose, or one day in ten, or two a week.
Bunyan argues that *time* is required to be set apart for the worship of God,
but under the new law of the gospel the precise time is not prefixed. And
the seventh-day Sabbath belongs, not to "natural theology" before the
time of Moses, but is part of that law on Sinai which is "the ministration
of death" and from which Christ has set Christians free.

One of the ironies of the controversy is that the seventh-day sabbatarians
sought to further the cause of good relations between Christians and Jews.
Bampfield was a Hebraist. Peter Chamberlen (1601–83) was a physician to
the first three Stuart kings and visited synagogues on the continent, and it
was claimed that some Jews shared worship with the sabbatarians and that
there was friendship with Rabbis. Bunyan, on the other hand, warns of
the danger of a return to repressive Judaism and to counter the advocated
obedience to the old law, describes the Jews as "Christ's deadliest enemies".
In 1909 Bunyan's book to which his adversaries did not reply at the time,
was attacked in a work by Walter Lancelot Holland, *Bunyan's Sabbatic*

Blunders. He maintained that one reason why the Church abandoned the seventh-day Sabbath was "a Satanic kind of hatred towards the Jews". He anticipates those modern expositors who detect anti-semitism in the New Testament, particularly in the gospels of Luke and John.[2]

Amid all this and his preaching beyond Bedford, notably in London, Bunyan published in 1686 *A Book for Boys and Girls*, "a new genre" for him, of which the first edition did not come to light until 1888. It was a book of poetry and emblems, in some ways already old-fashioned.[3]

It does, however, show what a rounded human being he was with a pen in his hand and the poetry of his soul flowing through it. There is but one aim, like that of the exiled Duke in Shakespeare's *As You Like It*, to find "sermons in stones and (God) in everything". This sometimes is overdone and contrasts dully with the humanity of *The Pilgrim's Progress* as when "the sight of a pound of candles falling to the ground" is to intimate "the bulk of God's elect in their lapsed state". But "On a Swallow" contains a truth of adult experience as well as lines children may understand; while pilgrims must always travel "with songs to Zion":

> This pretty bird! Oh how she flies and sings;
> But could she do so if she had not wings?
> Her wings bespeak my faith, her songs my peace;
> When I believe and sing, my doubtings cease.

Froude admired "Meditations upon an Egg":

> The egg's no chick by falling from a hen,
> No man's a Christian till he's born again;
> The egg's at first contained in the shell,
> Men afore grace in sin and darkness dwell;
> The egg, when laid, by warmth is made a chicken;
> And Christ by grace the dead in sin doth quicken;
> The egg when first a chick the shell's its prison,
> So flesh to soul who yet with Christ is risen.

Bunyan's controversial tone became somewhat more moderate in these years. He hoped the Seventh-Day Baptists would not "take it ill at my hand that I thus freely speak my mind". And his tender, passionate offer of the divine forgiveness was never more intense. Two of five works of his to be published in the months immediately before his death were *Good News for the Vilest of Men* and *The Advocateship of Jesus Christ*. The former is a discourse upon Luke 24:47, "And that repentance and remission of sins should be preached in his name among all nations, beginning at Jerusalem." The last phrase of the verse gives the work the title by which it has become best known, "The Jerusalem Sinner Saved". He describes Jerusalem as:

> the Shambles, the very Slaughter-shop for Saints. This was the place wherein the Prophets, Christ, and his People, were most horribly persecuted and murdered. Yea, so hardened at this time was this Jerusalem in her Sins, that she feared not to commit the biggest, and to bind herself by Wish under the guilt and damning evil of it; Saying when she had murdered the Son of God, His Blood be upon us and our Children.

This Jerusalem drove Christ out of the world.

Bunyan, we may think, paints Jerusalem in too uniform shades of dark. He does not attempt to understand the *realpolitick* of the condemnation of Jesus, that it could be depicted in the colours of classical tragedy. It is the simple truth that Christ was driven out, there was no room for him there, Jerusalem could not contain him. But this was the result of the compromises and expediencies to which politicians and statespersons have had to resort throughout all ages for what seems to be the general good. "It is expedient that one man should die for the people." Caiaphas may not have been a monster of wickedness as much as a statesman of mixed motives and utilitarian principles. One of the difficulties of evangelical Christianity with all its love and longing for souls is that out of its very compassion for sinners it needs absolute evil from which the sinner is rescued. And Bunyan has a point to make, deeply moving and totally evangelical: "That Jesus Christ would have mercy offered in the first place to the biggest Sinners."

This is "a help for despairing souls". We have noticed more than once Bunyan's concern with despair, from his own despair in *Grace Abounding* to that of Christian and Hopeful in Doubting Castle, and we have quoted from this treatise his apostrophes to dismiss the terrible state, which was so frequent in his time, caused alike by social and political conditions, and not least by Calvinist theology, which itself seemed to speak to the times because it reckoned with despair as a human state but also a *praeparatio evangelicae*.[4] Bunyan has a dilemma here because he believes that unless we despair of ourselves and of our own ability and efforts to secure salvation we shall indeed be damned; and yet despair is the state from which Christ sets us free. In *Good News* he seeks at once to arouse it "and then to channel it into a positive direction before it can lead to the neurotic or psychotic

113

states dominated by dread of reprobation".[5] He does not write as the Bunyan of *Grace Abounding* but more objectively, though as one who has been in despair with good reason. "I have been Vile *my self* . . . I speak not this to lessen my wickedness." He reminisces about his youth, his evil influence on other young people and the stir caused when he started seriously to go the church. His military experience and interests are evidenced in this example:

> I heard once a story from a Souldier, who with his company had laid Siege against a Fort, that so long as the Besieged were perswaded their foes would show them no favour, they fought like Madmen; but when they saw one of the fellows taken, and received to favour, they all came tumbling down from their Fortress, and delivered themselves into their Enemies' hands.

He concludes: "Let us, therefore, upon the sight of our wretchedness, fly and venturously leap into the Arms of Christ, which are now as open to receive us into his Bosom, as they were when nailed to the Cross." There is echo there, unconscious, of course, of one of the earliest liturgies much loved in the Roman Catholic and Anglican revisions of the Eucharistic Prayer. In the Anaphora of the apostolical tradition of Hippolytus it is said of Christ that he "stretched forth his hands for suffering", paraphrased in the Third Eucharistic Prayer of the Alternative Service Book, 1980 as "He opened wide his arms for us on the cross" and in Eucharistic Prayer II of the New Roman Missal, "For their sake he opened his arms on the cross." This indeed marks a whole tradition of devotion to the Crucified. Christ died in this way because on a cross one dies with outstretched arms.

But Bunyan has to deal yet again with the objection: *But how if I should have sinned the sin unpardonable, or That called the sin against the Holy Ghost.* He shows that the sign of this sin is a total vilifying of Jesus Christ, a repudiation of his Saviourhood, a refusal to come to him. The sin is the sin against the Spirit because the Holy Spirit testifies to Christ in Scripture and it is that testimony that is rejected when Christ is judged to be "an Impostor, a Magician, a Witch". This sin is unpardonable because the One who brings pardon is declared to be of Beelezebub, the Devil.

The Advocateship of Jesus Christ is written not for sinners but for the benefit of all believers. It displays considerable legal knowledge acquired from Bunyan's trial and imprisonment, the litigation of the age and his knowledge, through preaching visits and Nonconformist friendships, of the City of London. Its argument is simple, though the attempt to draw out the legal analogy may make it complex. The similitude does not always simplify. What Bunyan is saying from 1 John 2:1, "If any man sin we have an advocate with the Father, Jesus Christ the righteous", is that the elect, the adopted children of God, when through the machinations of the devil they seem to fall from grace, have Christ to plead their cause. He procures their acquittal by transferring his own righteousness to them. His advocacy succeeds his priesthood; the latter is his perpetual intercession by virtue of his sacrifice offered once for all; the former is the pleading of that sacrifice for those, the redeemed, who have fallen into sin, "as David, Joshua or Peter". He does this alone, not by proxy or intermediary. We have the supreme mediator the Son of God himself, but Bunyan does not here make anything of direct access to God through Jesus Christ; rather, he says, "it would lessen sin should it be removed by a Saint or an Angel; it would make the Advocateship of Jesus Christ superfluous, yea, needless should it be possible that sin could be removed from us by either Saint or Angel".

Richard L. Greaves has noted two intriguing details. "An Instance of God's terrible Judgement", as the second edition describes it in the list of contents, is taken from the life of Bruno of Cologne, Founder of the Carthusian Order, who died in 1101. In the text Bunyan does not mention Bruno or the source but simply writes:

I remember that somewhere I have read, as I think, concerning one, who when he was carrying upon Men's Shoulders to the Grave, cried out as he lay upon the Bier, *I am accused before the just Judgement of God*; and a while later *I am condemned before the just Judgement of God*.

The Contents Table in the first edition goes into more detail and cites a Latin source. The story is spread over the three days of the doctor's ("of great note for godliness") lying in church before burial and he rises on each day in turn and cries ever more dolefully as at the last he, judged and accused, is condemned. That this detailed narration and reference was omitted from the second edition may mean that it was originally a printer's insertion and that Bunyan, unwilling to publicise a Roman Catholic legend by a specific reference, insisted on its excision.

Greaves also calls attention to this passage: "I did use to be much taken with one Sect of Christians, for that it was usually their way, when they made mention of the Name of *Jesus* to call him, *the blessed King of Glory*. Christians should do thus; 'twould do them good."

The reference is to the Fifth-Monarchists, whom Bunyan in earlier days had found "appealing" though he never seems to have espoused their violence even when in the 1660s he was persecuted and in prison. It was their millenarian hopes and Apocalyptic expectations which for a time he shared in those tense days after the Restoration, and which he sought somewhat obliquely to restate in works written in the "Indian summer" of Fifth-Monarchism, 1682–5 and published posthumously, but which he has now abandoned. He now sees that suffering is a perpetual, if intermittent, condition of the people of God, rather than a portent of the end. But he looks back with some nostalgia to the millenarian hopes which saw some Christians through hard times and he loves their devotion to the titles of Christ. The use of the titles aids reverence, but more, not only enables us to think of him as exercising his various offices but makes us enquire by word and meditation and "of one another, *What there is in that Office*" and how it profits the Church.[6]

By the time Bunyan was in his late fifties the hopes of the Good Old Cause had totally faded. Bunyan and his co-religionists knew that attempted revolution had failed and that further rebellion was not likely to succeed, especially after the defeat of Monmouth in 1685. There had to be some partnership with the state, not perpetual opposition. In *Antichrist and His Ruin*, a late work published after his death, Bunyan declares that "*Antichrist shall not down but by the hand of Kings*. The Preacher then kills her Soul, and the King kills her Body."

There is some evidence that Bunyan was not unwilling to co-operate with James II after the new Declaration of Indulgence in April 1687. James reversed the Tory-Anglican policy of his brother's later years, a policy necessitated by the threat of popish plots and Anglican fear of James's accession, although Charles II himself was received, on his deathbed, into the Roman Church, where his true religious allegiance had always been. The intent of James's policy was to give opportunities to Catholics hitherto denied and he sought the support of Dissenters in order to further his aim of establishing an absolute Catholic monarchy, on the pattern of Louis XIV across the Channel. Bunyan must have been suspicious of the king's drift but he did not think it wrong to avail himself of the new liberty offered to Nonconformists after years of living under the persecution and adverse discrimination of Anglicans. Whether he was himself offered "a Place of Publick Trust" as alleged in the anonymous continuation of his life, appended to *Grace Abounding*, is not certain, but six of his church members served in the drastically remodelled Bedford Corporation, so that he could not have opposed the king's changes. Ecclesiologically, Nonconformists would seem to be Roman Catholics' fiercest foes; but there has more than once been a strange partnership, not unmixed with fellow-feeling, between those on the same side of the statutory gulf fixed between them and the privileged state Church.

Bunyan died untimely, before the crisis which overthrew James II and united Anglicans and Nonconformists had come fully to fruition. His premature death was due to an errand of mercy. In August 1688, *en route* to London, he went to Reading to try to reconcile a father with the son he threatened to disinherit. On continuing the ride to London he was soaked in a rainstorm; he did not seem to suffer more than a cold in the head and fulfilled a preaching engagement on 19th August. As a result he became seriously ill with a fever, probably pneumonia. He was bedridden at the house of John Strudwick, a grocer at the sign of the Star on Snow Hill. After ten days of suffering, borne with "much Constancy and Patience", he died, it is said on 31st August. He was buried in the Dissenters' graveyard, Bunhill Fields.

9

The Man: His Place in the History of Spirituality and in Our Times

The familiar portrait of John Bunyan "the Dreamer", prefixed to the third edition of *The Pilgrim's Progress* in 1679 and originating in a pencil drawing by Robert White, shows him aged fifty, a pleasant face, unlined, with a half-smile in repose and eyes not luminous, but honest, yet not perhaps over-confident. A contemporary wrote:

> In countenance, he appeared to be of a stern and rough temper [not quite what the portrait suggests], but in his conversation mild and affable; not given to loquacity or to much discourse in company unless some urgent occasion required it; observing never to boast of himself or his parts, but rather to seem low in his own eyes, and submit himself to the judgement of others; abhorring lying and swearing, being just, in all that lay in his power, to his word; not seeming to revenge injuries, loving to reconcile differences and make friendships with all. He had a sharp quick eye, with an excellent discerning of persons, being of good judgement and quick wit . . . He was tall of stature, strong-boned though not corpulent, somewhat of a ruddy face, with sparkling eyes, wearing his hair on his upper lip; his hair reddish, but in his later days time had sprinkled it with grey; his nose well set, but not declining or bending; his mouth moderate large, his forehead something high, and his habit always plain and modest.[1]

Bunyan is reticent about his family life, not giving his first wife's name, though not disowning his second, Elizabeth's, courage in pleading for him on his arrest. There is no doubt that he saw woman's true role as that of man's helpmeet. He seems to have been happy at home. Elizabeth outlived him, though his blind daughter by his first marriage had died while he was in prison. He refused to exploit his own fame for the advancement of his family's fortunes.

That fame was extensive. Part I of *The Pilgrim's Progress* in 1678 had a vast number of readers not only in this country but in Europe and New England. His preaching, especially in London, attracted large crowds. Twelve hundred people would assemble before seven o'clock on a dark winter's morning if he were preaching, and it is said that in Zoar Street, Southwark the meeting-house was at times so full that he had to be lifted into the pulpit over the people's heads. Many who came out of curiosity to hear the popular author who had no formal scholarship were not at ease that this unordained tinker should presume to dispense the word of God.[2] But some who came to scoff or "for novelty sake", "went away well satisfied with what they heard and wondered as the Jews did at the Apostles, viz. whence this Man should have these things".[3]

We may take the traditional view and ascribe this to genius, especially the writings, though historians have never been happy with the category of uniqueness, and the latest literary criticism recoils from the notion of authorial autonomy and regards works of wide popularity and status in the classical canon as equally the creation of their culture and their readers. Bunyan had more scholarship than he claims, but this derived from the Church, its leaders and its people, rather than from the schools. And there must have been a freshness in his very lack of Patristic references, as in Caroline Anglican sermons, or the scholastic teasings out of learned Puritan exegesis.

His understanding and interpretation of the Christian life come from his own humanity and experience, not from bloodless categories; from his desire for the living God and his fascination with people, not from iron, pre-mundane decrees. Their somewhat prudish audiences thought it daring when popular Edwardian expositors described *The Pilgrim's Progress* as a novel, but about Bunyan as a whole there is more than a moralist's interest in men and women, even though the condemnation of the unrighteous is without remission and those who trust in their own works and knowledge rather than in Christ, though virtuous, are, like Ignorance, consigned to hell even from the gate of heaven.

Underlying all is compassion, tenderness of heart. "Bowels becometh pilgrims." His own spiritual struggles made a man merciful by nature, more merciful still. And he was never over-confident. Christian nearly sinks in the river at the last. "I hope I know something of these things," he writes in the conclusion of *Grace Abounding*, when he describes the

119

paradoxes of the love of Christ with a tenderness not matched in T. S. Eliot, though which a certain type of Anglican might regard as a touch sentimental: "Of all tears, they are best that are made by the Blood of Christ; and of all joy, that is sweetest that is mixt with mourning over Christ; O 'tis a goodly thing to be on our knees with Christ in our arms before God."

"I *hope* I know something of these things", not "I know". He lives by what Vincent Newey has called "confiding uncertainty".[4]

He observes and loves human life as does the poet or artist who, according to that master of many distinguished Methodists of the period between the wars, W. R. Maltby (1865–1951), "cannot in the end help loving a thing so strange, piteous and enthralling as the story of every human soul must be".[5] This is not a quality for which all Christians, Calvinist, Arminian or Catholic, are necessarily distinguished.

There is an earthiness in Bunyan, at times even a coarseness, expressed in his vigorous yet musical Anglo-Saxon prose, which, though on a heavenward journey, keeps him close to the heart of human life. He uses the things about him in the world to describe eternal realities. Conversion comes upon him in roadways, doorways, shops and fields. "Walking brought him closer to heaven."[6] True in some of this he is no more than any English emblem writer and sometimes his "sermons in stones" are as conventional and unimaginative as any and, in Coleridge's famous distinction, the Bunyan of the Conventicle gets the better of the Bunyan of Parnassus.

He has a remarkable tolerance with regard to many of the disputes within Nonconformity, notably on baptism. In *The Heavenly Footman*, published in 1698 but generally regarded as a work of the first imprisonment and a precursor of *The Pilgrim's Progress*, he writes: "Here is one runs a *Quaking*, another a *Ranting*; one again runs after the *Baptism*, and another after the *Independency*; Here's one for *Free-will*, and another for *Presbytery*, and yet possibly all these Sects run quite the wrong way." He tells his readers to "fly *Seducers* Company, keep Company with the soundest Christians, that have most experience of Christ, and be sure thou have a care of *Quakers, Ranters, Free-willers*: Also do not have too much Company with some *Anabaptists*, though I go under that name myself."[7]

In *Peaceable Principles and True* (1674), his response to the violent attacks of Baptist authors on *Differences in Judgement about Water-Baptism*, he says he would be and hopes he is a *Christian*. "And as for those Factious Titles of *Anabaptists, Independents, Presbyterians*, or the like, I conclude, that they came neither from *Jerusalem*, nor *Antioch* but rather from *Hell* and *Babylon*;

for they naturally tend to divisions, *you may know them by their fruits.*"[8] His tolerance does not extend to Anglicans because theirs is state religion imposed by sanctions of government and not the freedom of the Spirit, which would preclude an imposed liturgy; and they include not only ritualistic and persecuting high churchmen, Laudians redivivi at the Restoration, but Latitudinarians.

This Bunyan with all his humanity and dislike of parties was steeped in Calvinism, and it is impossible to understand him apart from it even though at times in his emphasis on the human will, and his concern for sinners, he writes almost like an Arminian. Calvinism could be cruel and drive people to despair, as its mid-seventeenth-century opponents, and later John Wesley, knew, and as John Stachniewski in his terrifying indictment of Puritanism, *The Persecutory Imagination*, in which he seeks to reverse the vast rehabilitation of the last half a century of scholarship, has shown. Calvin himself foresaw the dangers:

> For there is scarcely a mind in which the thought does not sometimes arise. Whence your salvation but from the election of God? But what proof have you of your election? When once this thought has taken possession of any individual, it keeps him perpetually miserable, subjects him to dire torment, or throws him into a state of complete stupor.

Bunyan too, in *The Heavenly Footman*, warns against "prying overmuch into God's Secret Decrees", which could cause the person to stumble and fall to eternal overthrow.[9]

John Stachniewski gives a brilliant analysis of *Grace Abounding*,[10] which invokes sociology and modern literary criticism as well as theology in its interpretation. That Bunyan's despair was in part induced by the prevailing Calvinist ideology is unquestionable. And all through his life Bunyan believed that only a few would be saved. But his terrible struggles in the 1650s were, as the range of Stachniewski's scholarship shows, due to other factors as well, his social position and the class snobbery from which he suffered, the competition of so many confused and confusing sects for his soul, his comparison of himself with those who seemed to be true saints as well as the literalism with which at first he read Scripture and his regarding law and gospel as of equal authority. And we must not ignore the temperament of the creative artist.

That he came to understand that gospel has prior authority was surely an effect of his reading of Luther whose theology is of equal importance in his spiritual journey, if not more decisive for his Christianity, and which helped him to find a gracious God, as conformity to liturgy and Catholic discipline could not. And there is a prevailing optimism in his works, in spite of some of his dire warnings and Ignorance's consignment to hell. His work as a preacher may have fostered it, as well as his writing, for public and artistic expression of any kind brings peace to the mind tortured by creativity as well as introspection and no one interested in people and concerned for their welfare can be solely a prophet of doom. Imprisonment too brought exhilaration as well as at times despair. Calvinism itself had its positive side. Once saved one was saved for ever and the sovereignty of God would prevail over all evil in spite of persecutions and seemingly "truth for ever on the scaffold, wrong for ever on the throne". Above all, one was saved through a work not one's own. "Thy righteousness is in heaven." Salvation does not depend on feelings or moods, assessments of one's own condition or the changes and chances of a fleeting world, but on "Jesus Christ, the same yesterday, today and for ever".

Whether the *Spiritual Exercises* of Ignatius Loyola, contrasted so favourably by Stachniewski, following Harbison, with Protestant spirituality, would have delivered Bunyan is debatable. They did not save Gerard Manley Hopkins three hundred years on.[11] They would certainly have taken hold of his phenomenal imagination. In spite of Stachniewski's contention that in the glorification of free will they externalise the enemies of the soul instead of driving them inward to suicidal despair, their intensity might have caused Bunyan some agonising days and nights, though it is true that his own distress of spirit would be in some way identified with the passion of Christ. Yet in the end Christian's burden rolls away at the sight of that very cross encountered on the journey of faith. And it must not be forgotten that the *Exercises* were intended as instruments of a church authority which allowed freedom under severe restrictions and might have harried Bunyan as it did Teresa and, especially, John of the Cross and brought him to a worse persecution than he suffered.

A comparison with John of the Cross, to whom, incidentally, Stachniewski makes but one derogatory reference, which gives hint of a perception that this saint has affinities with Protestantism, is inevitable, not least because St John is not unlike Luther in some respects.[12] He believes that some experience of emptiness and of darkness must be undergone if the soul is to attain union with God and perceive creation through his eyes. Is "the valley of the shadow of death" the same as the "dark night of the soul"? It is doubtful if there was any Dionysian influence on Bunyan, though such mystical theology was in the mid-seventeenth-century air, witness John Everard and others who belonged to the Protestant under-world.[13] But Bunyan's is a different ethos and he would have been as critical of Everard's insistence on Christ within rather than without as he was of the Quakers'.

It is notable that Bunyan's valley has two parts, the second reputedly far more dangerous, but there is too little detail in his few paragraphs alongside the Spanish mystic's lengthy treatment to establish any corre-spondence with St John's night of the senses and night of the spirit. For both, however, God is all and to be desired above all, and the soul's journey is to lead to the beatitude of the divine love, though Bunyan's is realised in the communal life of a city. Both knew agonising spiritual struggles, a Lutheran *anfechtung* (dereliction), and believed that this was in some sense necessary to salvation. Both knew persecution from fellow-Christians; their great works came out of imprisonment, though the Car-melite's was both shorter and more harsh; both were steeped in Scripture, though they did not dwell on the same passages; both were insistent on faith and a stripping of the confidence of the natural man and the conven-tional exercises and achievements of devotion, which may be the deepest of pitfalls; both insisted than Christ could not be sought without the cross, and for both darkness is at once the most terrifyingly dangerous and the most illuminating of experiences. Bunyan quotes Job 12:22 that God "discovereth deep things out of darkness, and bringeth out to light the shadow of death". There is more clutter of snares, gins, traps in Bunyan's dark valley. His is the way one might have to tread on a foul night in Bedfordshire woods and fields. For John of the Cross the way is the ascent of a pitiless Spanish mountain, the desolation is the appalling absence of God. But Bunyan's Christian knows mental confusion even as John of the Cross's pilgrim may feel vacant of mind and incapable of coherence.

As Christian goes on the day breaks and there is light at last to see him safely through. Even then as he journeys he will be assailed at times by melancholy and imprisoned by despair; but there is joy too, strengthening companionship, the beauty now and then of the way itself, the vision of the glory of his goal and the promises which assure him that these very tribulations are the tokens that he is set on course for the kingdom of God.

Some similarities may be discerned between Bunyan's spirituality and that of the Desert Fathers and its influence on western Christianity through Gregory the Great. There is in Bunyan what Gregory calls "Compunc-tion", the divine piercing and goading, and "the gift of tears". Bunyan would have understood better than modern Methodists a verse of Charles Wesley's, even though he would not have endorsed the implied perfectionism of the stanzas which follow:

> Deepen the wound thy hands have made
>   In this weak helpless soul;
> Till mercy with its kindly aid,
>   Descends to make me whole.

Bunyan's pilgrims, in spite of their joyous dances, are always in some sense the walking wounded. There is no "perfect cure" in this world, as Wesley believed; yet the mystery of the divine love may be known, as Bunyan makes plain in his posthumously published exposition of Ephesians 3:18–19. Certainly for Bunyan the soul must be wounded, the heart enlarged to breaking point before mercy can do its perfect work. And there are tears. They are necessary to repentance. The water often stands in Christian's eyes. There is no *apatheia* as he considers the way he has been led, the perils from which he has been delivered, the sins and weaknesses and lack of faith to which he has been prone all along, and above all the infinite mercy which saves sinners, the vilest sinners, at such tremendous cost. There are tears of joy as well as of grieving. This is not far from the Orthodox conception of the second baptism – the baptism of tears.

There is also reference in Bunyan to Enlightenment. He derives this from Hebrews 6:4, 5 and 10:32 where it seems to refer to Christian initiation, though in passages of warnings both of the unforgivable sin of apostasy and the tribulations which follow on being made a Christian. "Enlightenment" is Justin Martyr's term for entry into the Christian life sealed by baptism, and an element in the spirituality of the desert.[14]

Bunyan does write out of a world different from ours, though, as we have noticed at the beginning, Christopher Hill finds a message for the Third World of our time and the poor, who are always with us. Bunyan is always on the side of the socially inferior and those spurned with contempt by the rich and ruling. And those who find relevance in Apocalyptic for today's world will not regard him as simply to be a subject for the more abstruse PhD theses. Yet he was no great political activist. He would not be silenced from his preaching when the alternative was imprisonment, which might have led to transportation or death, and which removed him for long periods from his needy family. But his work was mostly pastoral and preaching and his later arguments were more with those he believed to be Christians in error than with the state; more to guide the little flock on their way to heaven than to advocate radical measures to ease their lot on earth. There are no calls to arms. He is neither liberation theologian nor freedom fighter. In *Seasonable Counsel; or Advice to Sufferers*, a supplement to *The Holy War*, he "made it clear that in times of persecution the saints could do no more than patiently suffer and pray to God for deliverance from evil rulers. In this tract Bunyan expressed one of his profoundest insights; the necessity for Christians to suffer *actively* for righteousness but *willingly* embracing affliction."[15]

The chief question for our time is whether Bunyan's view of the universe has any meaning for us. In 1663, in the style of William Perkins, the Elizabethan Puritan, he produced a "Mapp: Shewing the Order and Causes of Salvation and Damnation". An equilateral triangle at the top represents God the Trinity. (There is an interesting comparison with John Piper's tapestry in Chichester Cathedral, where the Trinity is also depicted by an equilateral triangle, but in bright red.) The reprobate's chart, in black lines, is on the right facing; the way of salvation on the left. In circles is a whole theology of salvation and damnation, starting with the covenant of grace on the one hand and the covenant of works on the other, leading to the ways of election or reprobation. John Stachniewski, who regards it as an example of all that is most frightening and ambiguous in Calvinistic Puritanism, comments:

> Conviction(s) for sin(ne) appears under both election and reprobation. The reprobate have "desires after life" and some "taste" of Life; but while the elect gain in confidence the reprobate soul "groweth secure". The elect "Soul is cast down" and tempted to despair; the reprobate soul, by supposed contrast, completes its preparation for hell with "The sinne against the Holy Ghost" which gives rise to "a certain fearfull looking for Judgement". Although Bunyan's terms are biblical quotations they are stacked up in a way that gives them a cumulative impact their original contexts do not support.[16]

Some people are helped by maps even if they do not correspond to the actual terrain to be traversed. In *Bugles and a Tiger* John Masters told of a Gurkha prisoner of the Japanese in Burma, who managed to escape and made his way by an arduous journey through the Burmese jungle back to base. They asked him how he had done it. He said he had a map. Astonished and eager they asked to see it. He produced it. It was a street map of London.

There are those who may live good and Christian lives and attain health and peace of soul according to a plan of salvation which does not bear any relation to what seem to most people be the objective and believable realities of God and the world. And though it may be fearsome it may lead, as with Bunyan, to a life of integrated fulfilment and at any rate a sight of journey's end. But – to borrow a comparison used many years ago by B. H. Streeter in a different context – most of us gain more help for the spiritual life from a Turner than from a Baedeker. Or from a story than a chart; from Bunyan's *The Pilgrim's Progress* than from his "Mapp".[17]

Life is a story, the story of a journey. It demands choices and these are not as autonomous as we suppose; they are conditioned by social and heredity factors, sometimes it would seem by chance or even the stars. Belief in divine election is not wholly untrue to human experience if there is initial faith that the story has a meaning and the journey an end, if we turn it into a pilgrimage, a concept which, in our time, should unite all Christians, even if there are some disagreements and contentions on the way. And if one is preserved from evil and kept in the way of goodness and the love of friends, this will seem to be a mystery and undeserved; "the wonder, Why such love to me?" Some, not all, may have heavy burdens and be desperate to have them removed. The burdens will be there because of the real troubles of life, a hyper-sensitivity, some feeling of guilt due to mistakes or misdeeds, or a belief, not always created by a harsh religious system, in a jealous and vengeful God. The vicissitudes of the journey will bring troubles, traumas and tensions to almost all, whether or not they begin with a burden.

For the Christian the journey brings all the travellers, all the characters in the story, to the cross. Not all will find from it the same meaning. For some it may be the assurance that God is gracious and I am accepted just as I am. Others may believe that there God has done for me what I cannot do for myself, reversed the past, and that he has released his own life through death for me so that I may "put on" Christ, and when God looks at me he sees Christ, me as I may become, just as, in Max Beerbohm's story *The Happy Hypocrite*, the ravaged gallant, Lord George Hell, wears the mask of a handsome man to win his lady and becomes transformed into its likeness.

Others may see in the cross the suffering God, taking upon himself the consequences of his creation, bearing the burdens of his own universe, his power and glory seen only in sacrificial love until his work of salvation is complete. And then the power in its victorious fullness!

Again there are those like St Paul, who would say that we ourselves must be crucified with Christ, our sins nailed to his tree. We must see the world and ourselves from the perspective of Calvary and of a crucified God. We must take up the cross after Christ. This is what discipleship means and from henceforth the journey is following Christ finding our place in his story.

This is a way of understanding union with Christ in the sense in which Bunyan was led into its mystery. It is not mystic absorption or identity. It is not *theosis*, deification, as with the Orthodox and Lancelot Andrewes and an Anglican tradition.[18]

There is still the endless qualitative distance, in Kierkegaard's phrase. And yet the Holy Spirit joins us in a union of wills as close as that of bread and eater, vine and branches, or even as the union of Persons in the Godhead.[19]

There will still be sins in our lives. We shall never outgrow the oldest and lowliest of all prayers, "God be merciful to me a sinner", and we must never be complacent or self-satisfied. This is why, in *The Holy War*, Diabolians still lurk in the City of Mansoul. John Wesley differed from Bunyan and the Calvinists here. For him, although we must press on to perfection, which may be attained in this life, "a gracious soul may fall from grace". For Bunyan the chosen will persevere unto the end and believe that Christ, the Advocate, eternally pleads their cause. When Oliver Cromwell was dying he asked his chaplain Thomas Goodwin if it were possible to fall from grace. Goodwin assured him that it was not. And the Protector died in peace because he said, looking back over all the compromises and moral failures of the statesman, "I know I was in grace once." And some of us may cling to that, even though we shall want the Prayer Book's "words of such terrible weight"[20] said over us at the last:

> Thou knowest, Lord, the secrets of our hearts; shut not thy merciful ears to our prayer; but spare us Lord most holy, O God most mighty, O holy and merciful Saviour, thou most worthy Judge eternal, suffer us not at our last hour for any pains of death to fall from thee.

And what of the goal of the journey? A pilgrimage is a journey with a goal. Bunyan pictures it in the images of the Revelation of John, the city which the elect pilgrims reach immediately after they have crossed the river of death. For centuries Christians believed in this Celestial City and sang about it. For us death seems more than ever a passage to nothingness as time goes on and population and physiological knowledge alike increase. The mind cannot conceive of the conditions of a life beyond this which

127

does not seem to be a combination of fantasy and wishful thinking, incompatible with what we know of life and death. Buddhism has its appeal, the drop of water lost yet preserved in the vast ocean of the infinite; reincarnation is once more taken seriously, a depressing belief and not, in spite of some valiant attempts to reconcile it, compatible with Christianity. The City of Gold, the choirs, the trumpets seem naïve – what music will they play from our one yet culturally divided world? F. R. Leavis, however, in a fine piece, had this to say:

> However naïvely Bunyan as a pastor might have talked of the eternal life as the reward that comes after death to the Christian who has persevered through the pains and trials of his earthly pilgrimage, the sense of the eternal conveyed by *The Pilgrim's Progress* and coming from the whole man ("trust the tale", as Lawrence said, not the writer) is no mere matter of a life going on and on for ever that starts after death. It is a sense of a dimension felt in the earthly life – in what for us *is* life, making this something that transcends the time succession, transience and evanescence and gives significance.[21]

And there are times when in our human journey we stand like Christian and Hopeful on the Delectable Mountains and though we hold the perspective glass in trembling hands, we may think we see something like the gate and also some of the glory of the place.

It is not naïve to think that at times like this we have prevision of a reality beyond time, what Boethius called "the possession of unlimited life all at once".

The notion of a Celestial City is important because it gives hope of an eternal life that is not solitary but communal, shared with others in the love of God. And there is the promise also in Scripture and in Bunyan of a face-to-face vision of God, no longer through a glass darkly. This is 1 Corinthians 13:12. There is also, "His servants shall serve (worship) him and they shall see his face" (Revelation 22:3b, 4) a text given to me by an Evangelical rector long ago, on parting from my first church.

This is occupying the attention of David Ford, Regius Professor of Divinity at Cambridge, who has written in a learned essay of "the face of Christ" (2 Corinthians 4: 6). He could almost devise a whole theology from meditation on it and believes that:

> it can help us to rethink many ideas of eschatology. If the ultimate is recognised in a face, we glimpse a way out of the dilemma of eschatology, which so often seems unable to conceive of a definitive

consummation of history without also seeing it as predetermined. The face of Christ is definitive but it does not predetermine. Rather it is the counterpart of a new history of freedom and responsibility, involving a new notion of what glory and freedom are.[22]

Those are words of modern technical theology and hardly in the style of Bunyan. But if we revise our understanding of God in the light of the glory seen on the cross we may think of the goal of our pilgrimage, the end, yet not the end, of our story as does Mr Standfast. "I am going now to see that Head that was crowned with thorns and that Face that was spit upon for me"; or with Charles Wesley, of "that dear disfigured face". And yet it is the face which is also radiant with the divine Glory, the face of him who is not only the Christ of Golgotha but the Christ of the Transfiguration, who comes from the East where the sun rises and the little children are; whose face if ever we see it we shall recognise because it bears some of the features of our friends.[23]

Abbreviations

Mr Badman	John Bunyan, *The Life and Death of Mr Badman*
Conventicle and Parnassus	N. H. Keeble, ed., *John Bunyan: Conventicle and Parnassus*, Clarendon Press, Oxford, 1988
DNB	*The Dictionary of National Biography*, 1908–9 edn
GA	John Bunyan, *Grace Abounding to the Chief of Sinners*, ed. Roger Sharrock, Oxford, 1962
Hall	Basil Hall, 'Puritanism: the problem of definition' in *Humanists and Protestants*, Clark, 1990
Hill	Christopher Hill, *A Turbulent, Seditious and Factious People: John Bunyan and his church*, Clarendon Press, Oxford, 1988
HW	John Bunyan, *The Holy War*, ed. Roger Sharrock and James F. Forrest, Oxford, 1980
Misc. Works	*The Miscellaneous Works of John Bunyan*, gen. ed. Roger Sharrock, 12 vols, 1976ff.
PP	John Bunyan, *The Pilgrim's Progress*, ed. Roger Sharrock, Oxford, 1966
Reason, Grace and Sentiment	Isabel Rivers, *Reason, Grace and Sentiment: a study of the language of religion and ethics in England 1660–1780*, vol. I, Cambridge University Press, 1991
Stachniewski	John Stachniewski, *The Persecutory Imagination: English puritanism and the literature of religious despair*, Clarendon Press, Oxford, 1991
Works	*The Works of John Bunyan*, ed. George Offor, 3 vols, Glasgow, Edinburgh and London, 1860–2

Notes

1 Introduction

1 e.g. E. Allison Peers's edn of his complete works, 3 vols, rev. 1953; and his exposition in *Studies of the Spanish Mystics*, I, 2nd edn, 1951, and *Spirit of Flame*, SCM, 1979; E. W. Trueman Dicken, *The Crucible of Love*, DLT, 1963; Gerald Brenan, *St John of the Cross: his life and poetry*, CUP, 1973; Colin P. Thompson, *The Poet and the Mystic*, OUP, 1977.

2 see, e.g., the Macmillan Casebook on *The Pilgrim's Progress*, ed. Roger Sharrock, 1976.

3 see N. H. Keeble's summary, "The modern Bunyan" in *Conventicle and Parnassus*, pp. 260ff. For deconstructive treatment, see Stanley E. Fish, *Self-consuming Artifacts*, repr. Berkeley and Los Angeles, 1974; and a most thought-provoking essay by Graham Ward, "To be a reader: Bunyan's struggle with the language of Scripture in *Grace Abounding*", *Literature and Theology*, March 1990.

4 Hill, p. 368.

5 ibid. p. 375.

6 cf. E. P. Thompson, *The Making of the English Working Class*, Penguin, 1968, p. 34.

7 Alexander Whyte, *Bunyan Characters*, Three Series, Oliphant, Anderson and Ferrier, Edinburgh and London, many repr. from 1890s.

8 Henri Talon, *John Bunyan: the man and his works*, tr. Barbara Wall, London, 1972, p. 2200 n. 270.

9 G. F. Nuttall, *The Holy Spirit in Puritan Faith and Experience*, 1946, p. 9. For what precedes, see Hall, pp. 237–54. Hall points out that the term "Anglican" is not seventeenth-century: Laudians called themselves "Protestants", as the Archbishop himself did on the scaffold (p. 252 n. 26); while Baxter spoke of them as "the new prelatical way" (Nuttall, p. 9).

10 Hall, p. 254; G. S. Wakefield, *Puritan Devotion*, Epworth, 1957, pp. 111–29; H. R. McAdoo, *The Structure of Caroline Moral Theology*, Longmans, 1949; Thomas Wood, *English Casuistical Divinity*, SPCK, 1952.
11 Louis Dupré and Don E. Saliers, *Christian Spirituality*, III, Crossroads, New York, 1989, SCM, London, 1990, pp. 257–94; and in an essay in Kenneth Stevenson and Bryan Spinks, eds, *The Identity of Anglican Worship*, Mowbray, 1991.

2   Early Life and Times

1 GA 16.
2 N. H. Keeble, *The Literary Culture of Nonconformity in Later Seventeenth-Century England*, Leicester, 1987, p. 8 and refs.
3 J. F. McGregor and B. Reay, eds, *Radical Religion in the English Revolution*, OUP, 1986, p. 129.
4 Misc Wks, I, 213.
5 cf. Reay, op. cit. pp. 152f. For the sad case of blasphemy see Geoffrey F. Nuttall, *James Nayler: a fresh approach* (Friends Historical Society 1951).
6 Hill, pp. 55ff.
7 Isabel Rivers, "Bunyan and Restoration Latitudinarianism" in *Conventicle and Parnassus*, pp. 46f.
8 H. R. Trevor-Roper, *Archbishop Laud*, 1940, p. 188.
9 C. J. Stranks, *Anglican Devotion*, SCM, 1961, p. 63.
10 Hill, pp. 63f.
11 V. Newey, "Bunyan, experience and interpretation" in *Conventicle and Parnassus*, p. 195.
12 Peter Brown, *Augustine of Hippo*, Faber, 1967.
13 Sharrock, Introd. to GA, pp. xxvii–xxviii; cf. Newey, op. cit. p. 191.
14 Charles Péguy, "Victor Marie Comte Hugo" in *Oeuvres complètes de Charles Péguy*, Paris, 1916–55, XI, 121, qu. in Henri Talon, op. cit.
15 Richard L. Greaves, "The nature of the Puritan tradition" in R. Buick Knox, ed., *Reformation, Conformity and Dissent: essays in honour of Geoffrey Nuttall*, Epworth, 1977, p. 262.
16 GA 120, 121.
17 This is Father Victor White's gloss, which I owe to Richard Roberts in Kenneth Surin, ed., *Christ, Ethics and Tragedy: essays in honour of Donald MacKinnon*, Cambridge, 1989, p. 4.
18 Ray Monk, *Ludwig Wittgenstein: the duty of genius*, Cape, 1990, pp. 64f.
19 GA 4.

20 ibid. 8.

21 ibid. 12.

22 ibid. 37, 38.

23 ibid. 53–6.

24 ibid. 89–92.

25 ibid. 68.

26 ibid. 71.

27 ibid. 253–4.

28 ibid. 96–7.

29 ibid. 106.

30 ibid. 77–9.

31 ibid. 123–5.

32 ibid. 180.

33 see, e.g., Hall, pp. 208–36; Bunyan is a surprising omission from p. 235.

34 GA 129.

35 ibid. 130.

36 ibid. 158.

37 ibid. 163. For the effect of Spira on many in seventeenth-century England see Stachniewski, pp. 37ff.

38 ibid. 164.

39 ibid. 204.

40 ibid. 214.

41 ibid. 233.

42 Walter Marshall, *The Gospel Mystery of Sanctification*, 1692, pp. 51, 69.

3   Preacher and Controversialist

1 GA 265–8.

2 ibid. 268.

3 ibid. 276.

4 see H. I. Marrou, *A History of Education in Antiquity*.

5 PP, 162.

6 cf. McAdoo, op. cit.

7 see Peter Toon, *God's Statesman: the life and work of John Owen*, Exeter, 1971, p. 162; John Asty, "Memoirs of the life of John Owen", preface in *A Completion Collection of the Sermons of John Owen*, 1721, p. xxx; *Theology*, January–February 1991.

8 *Works*, III, p. 464.

9 Owen, *Works*, XVI, p. 319.

10 Misc. Works, I, p. 30. For Lloyd George see the story in Harold Macmillan, *The Past Masters*, Macmillan, 1975, pp. 55f., of his wanting

to say in a speech intended in reconciliation that he had made Herbert
Samuel the first Procurator of Palestine since Pontius Pilate.

11 *Works*, III, p. 767.

12 cf. Gordon Campbell, "Bunyan and the theologians" in *Conventicle
and Parnassus*, pp. 136ff.

13 cf. Augustine, *Confessions*, III, 3.

14 Misc. Works, I, 324–5.

15 The view of Adolf Jülicher, C. H. Dodd and others that the parables
must not be interpreted as allegories is now much challenged.

16 John R. Knott, jun. in *Conventicle and Parnassus*, p. 163. This discussion
is much indebted to his ch. "Bunyan and the Bible" and to
Campbell's "Bunyan and the theologians".

17 Andrew Louth, *Discerning the Mystery*, Clarendon Press, 1983, pp.
96–131.

18 William Perkins, *Works*, II, Cambridge, 1616, pp. 670, 673.

19 Roger Pooley, "Language and loyalty: plain style at the Restoration",
Literature and History. See also id. "Bunyan and style: plain and
simple" in *Conventicle and Parnassus*; and Keeble, *Literary Culture*, op.
cit. ch. 8.

20 Sharrock in Misc. Works, I, 304.

21 *Works*, II, p. 702.

22 Misc. Works, VIII, p. 342; I, 304, 311. For medieval personification
of Bible words, often ignorantly fanciful and grotesquely erroneous,
see Charles Smyth, *The Art of Preaching*, SPCK, 1940.

23 Misc. Works, XI, pp. 65–6.

24 ibid. I, 301.

25 *Works*, II, p. 127.

26 Misc. Works, XI, 80.

27 ibid. 52.

28 ibid. I, pp. 19–20.

29 Edward Burrough, *Works*, 1672, pp. 136–52, 275–309.

30 Roger Pooley in *Conventicle and Parnassus*, p. 105.

31 see e.g. E. P. Sanders, *Paul and Palestinian Judaism* (London 1977); and
Paul, Oxford Past Masters series (1991).

32 see Jerald C. Brauer in *Church History*, XXIII (June 1954), p. 104.

33 For John Dod see William Haller, *The Rise of Puritanism*, Columbia,
1938, passim.

34 Misc. Works, II, p. 147.

35 *On Englishing the Bible*, London, 1949, p. 11.

36 Kenneth Grayston, *Dying We Live: a new enquiry into the death of Christ
in the New Testament*, London, 1990, App. B, pp. 378–9.

37 Richard L. Greaves in Misc. Works, II, p. xxx; John Saltmarsh, *Free
Grace*, 1645, pp. 146–7; Misc. Works, IV, p. xxx; ibid. II, pp. 173–4.

38 John Wesley, *Journal*, V, pp. 243f. "Mr Law" is William Law, famed author of *A Serious Call to a Devout and Holy Life*, who later became influenced by the mysticism of Jacob Boehme, and with whom Wesley, earlier his disciple, had quarrelled on evangelical issues.

39 Misc. Works, p. 182.

40 cf. Karl Rahner, *Theological Investigations*, III, pp. 321–54.

41 cf. the hymn of Henry Twells, "Not for our sins alone/thy mercy Lord we sue".

42 Misc. Works, II, pp. 184–5.

43 Donald MacKinnon, *Borderlands of Theology*, London, 1968, p. 119.

44 cf. Rowan Williams in K. Surin, ed., *Christ, Ethics and Tragedy*, Cambridge, 1989, pp. 85ff.

45 Misc. Works, II, pp. 206, 209–10.

4   The Uses of Imprisonment

1 Nuttall, op. cit. p. 127; and for a discussion of the whole subject of tolerance in Puritanism, ibid. pp. 102–33.

2 For a summary study of witchcraft in the seventeenth century see Lawrence Stone, *The Past and the Present*, Routledge and Kegan Paul, 1981, ch. 8; and Keith Thomas, *Religion and the Decline of Magic*, the definitive work.

3 cf. Hugh Trevor-Roper, *Catholics, Anglicans and Puritans*, 1989 edn, p. 118.

4 see *A Relation of the Imprisonment of Mr John Bunyan*, Oxford, 1966, passim; and "A brief account of the author's imprisonment" app. to GA, p. 103.

5 see F. Heiler, *Prayer: a study in the history and psychology of religion*, Oxford, 1932, abr. tr. of *Das Gebet*, Munich, 5th edn, 1923; cf. *Concilium 1990/3*, "Asking and thanking".

6 Misc. Works, II, 247–8.

7 ibid. pp. 252, 269f.

8 ibid. pp. 269, 281–6.

9 GA 321.

10 *Works*, II, 446.

11 "The shadow of St Theresa or St John of the Cross never fell upon them so as to divert their reason into paroxysms of love", C. A. Patrides, ed., *The Cambridge Platonists*, Cambridge, 1980, p. 17. For difficulties involved in using the label "Cambridge Platonists" see *Reason, Grace and Sentiment*, pp. 28f.

12 For Fowler see *The Design of Christianity*, 1671, I, p. 6; V, pp. 36–7; XIX, pp. 221, 225–6; and for the dispute with Bunyan, Isabel Rivers,

"Bunyan and Restoration Latitudinarianism" in *Conventicle and Parnassus*, ch. 3; for imputed righteousness see G. S. Wakefield, "Bunyan and the Christian life" in ibid. pp. 132f.; and below, p. 126.

13 *Works*, II, 329, 322, 332.

14 qu. in Keeble, *Richard Baxter: Puritan man of letters*, Clarendon Press, Oxford, 1982, p. 24.

15 *Conventicle and Parnassus*, p. 69.

5 Bunyan and his Church

1 see H. G. Tibbutt, ed., *The Minutes of the First Independent Church (now Bunyan Meeting) at Bedford 1656 to 1766*. Publications of the Bedfordshire Historical Record Society, 55, Bedford, 1976.

2 Hill, pp. 92f.

3 Misc. Works, II, 244.

4 *Works*, I, 758.

5 PP 305.

6 ibid. p. 52.

7 Ignatius, "To the Ephesians", XX.2 in *The Apostolic Fathers*, tr. Francis Glimm, Joseph Marique and Gerald Welsh, New York, 1947, repr. 1969, p. 95.

8 see G. B. Harrison, ed., *The Narrative of the Persecution of Agnes Beaumont in 1674*, 1929; Gordon Rupp, "A Devotion of Rapture in English Puritanism" in R. Buick Knox, ed., *Reformation, Conformity and Dissent*, Epworth, 1977, p. 129; G. F. Nuttall, *Visible Saints*, Blackwell, 1957, p. 109. For Bunyan's repudiation of charges that he was a womaniser see GA 306ff,; and below, p. 110f.

9 cf. B. R. White in *Conventicle and Parnassus*, p. 9.

10 see Nuttall, *Visible Saints*, pp. 119ff.

11 For documentation see T. L. Underwood, ed. in Misc. Works, IV, p. xxvi n. 28.

12 Misc. Works, IV, 226.

13 ibid. p. 186.

14 Nuttall, *Visible Saints*, p. 163, quoting S. C. Neill, *The Christian Society*, 1952.

6 The Pilgrim's Progress Part I

1 For Joyce's *Ulysses* see Frank Kermode, *An Appetite for Poetry*, Collins, 1989, pp. 201–15, 221–3.

2 J. G. Davies, *Pilgrimage Yesterday and Today: Why? Where? How?* SCM, 1988, pp. 107f.

3 Dag Hammerskjold, *Markings*, Faber, 1964.

4 A. F. Segal, *Paul the Convert*, Yale University Press, 1990.

5 Roger Sharrock, "Bunyan and the English emblem writers", *Review of English Studies*, 21 (1945), p. 111.

6 Simon Patrick, *A Further Continuation and Defence, or The Third Part of the Friendly Debate*, in *Works*, ed. Taylor, VI, II, qu. in *Reason, Grace and Sentiment*, p. 129, to which this part of the discussion is much indebted.

7 Rivers, ibid. p. 128.

8 see Keeble, "Bunyan and his reputation" in *Conventicle and Parnassus*, pp. 241ff.

9 cf. T. W. Manson, *The Teaching of Jesus*, Cambridge, 1931, passim.

10 cf. Stachniewski, p. 179.

11 Robert Bridges, "Bunyan's *The Pilgrim's Progress*", 1905, in Sharrock, ed., Macmillan Casebook series, pp. 107ff. Hill, p. 302, seems to take a not dissimilar view.

12 Keeble, *Literary Culture*, p. 239; for a view much more critical of Bunyan and of Christian see Hill, p. 300.

13 Henri Talon, *John Bunyan: the man and his works*, p. 144.

14 For literature on the subject and various attempted suicides see Hill, pp. 185ff.; Stachniewski, passim.

15 *Works*, III, p. 386.

16 U. Milo Kaufmann in *Conventicle and Parnassus*, p. 174.

17 cf. Hill, pp. 223ff.

18 George Steiner, *Real Presences*, Faber, 1989, p. 231.

19 "Many of Christian's lapses can be seen as failures of memory," John R. Knott, jun. in *Conventicle and Parnassus*, p. 167.

20 Misc. Works, XI, 65.

21 *Conventicle and Parnassus*, p. 67.

22 Kaufmann in ibid. p. 173.

23 I do not reckon this to be a christianising of the Charon myth, *pace* John A. T. Robinson, *On Being the Church in the World*, 1960, p. 131.

24 from the medieval carol *In dulci jubilo*.

7   *Three Later Books*

1 *Mr Badman*, pp. 2, 5, x.

2 ibid. p. 9.

3 J. A. Froude, *Bunyan*, p. 104.

4 *Mr Badman*, p. 35.

5 in *Conventicle and Parnassus*, p. 187.
6 ibid. p. 180 n. 22.
7 Froude, p. 133.
8 ibid. p. 147.
9 HW, pp. 249–50.
10 ibid. p. 207.
11 ibid. p. 246.
12 Froude, p. 171.
13 in *Conventicle and Parnassus*, p. 178.
14 Stachniewski, pp. 207–8, 184.
15 ibid. pp. 193ff.

8   The Last Years

1 see Hill, pp. 296ff.; T. L. Underwood in Misc. Works, IV, pp. xxxviiff.; also GA 315; Misc Works, XI, 81; Offer, II, 431.
2 see Underwood in Misc. Works, IV, p. liv.
3 see Sharrock in *Conventicle and Parnassus*, p. 72 and n.
4 cf. Stachniewski.
5 Richard L. Greaves in Misc. Works, XI, p. xxiv.
6 Misc. Works, XI, pp. xxxviff., 214, 108, 194.

9   The Man: His Place in the History of Spirituality and in Our Times

1 This is often quoted in older lives without reference. John Brown, *John Bunyan*, London 1887, p. 399, attributes it to George Cokoyn, a London minister.
2 e.g. Samuel Wesley, father of John and Charles, cited in *Reason, Grace and Sentiment*, p. 107.
3 "A continuation of Mr Bunyan's life" in GA 171.
4 GA, Conclusion 5; *Conventicle and Parnassus*, p. 197.
5 W. R. Maltby, qu. in R. Newton Flew, *The Idea of Perfection in Christian Theology*, Oxford, 1934, pp. 340–1.
6 Patricia Caldwell, *The Puritan Conversion Narrative*, Cambridge, 1983, p. 24.
7 Misc. Works, V, 152–3.
8 ibid. IV, p. 270.
9 Calvin, *Institutes*, III, xxiv.; Misc. Works, V, 156; qu. in Newey, *Conventicle and Parnassus*, p. 197.

10 Stachniewski, pp. 127–68.

11 see Richard Bernard Martin, *Gerard Manley Hopkins*, HarperCollins, 1991, especially chapters XIX and XX.

12 see, e.g., Rowan Williams, *The Wound of Knowledge*, Darton, Longman and Todd, 1979, p. 159.

13 For Everard see Wakefield, *A Dictionary of Christian Spirituality*; and DNB.

14 Justin Martyr, *The First Apology,* var. trs and edns; cf. Alan Jones, *Soul Making: the desert way of spirituality*, 1986, p. 86.

15 Richard L. Greaves in *Conventicle and Parnassus*, p. 40; Misc. Works, X, p. xx.

16 Stachniewski, p. 90.

17 cf. B. H. Streeter, *Reality*, Macmillan, 1926, p. 31.

18 see A. M. Allchin, *Participation in God*, Darton, Longman and Todd, 1988.

19 see above, p. 27.

20 Iris Murdoch, *An Unofficial Rose*, Penguin 1964, p. 14.

21 in Sharrock, ed., Casebook ser., p. 218.

22 Kenneth Surin, ed., *Christ, Ethics and Tragedy: essays in honour of Donald MacKinnon*, Cambridge, 1989, p. 127.

23 The last sentence echoes phrases from two Reformed theologians of the 1930s, Nathaniel Micklem and David Cairns.

Index

141